TWO HEBREW PROPHETS

TWO HEBREW PROPHETS

Studies in Hosea and Ezekiel

By

H. WHEELER ROBINSON

*Late Principal Emeritus of Regent's Park College,
Oxford, and Speaker's Lecturer in the
University of Oxford*

LUTTERWORTH PRESS
LONDON

7403

First published 1948
Second impression 1959
Third impression 1962
Fourth impression 1964

Printed in Great Britain by
Lowe and Brydone (Printers) Limited
London, N.W.10

Editorial Note

"In the last resort, it is in the prophetic consciousness and its continuance in personal religion that there is found the ultimate sanctuary in which the voice of God is still heard, the sanctuary in which the ancient Scriptures are still transferred into His living oracles." In these words, written at the end of his life, Dr. Wheeler Robinson gave expression to the faith that had sustained him through many years of specialized Old Testament study. They will be found illustrated again and again in the lectures which follow.

Those on Hosea were given in 1935 at a Summer School for former students of Regent's Park College. Dr. Wheeler Robinson had hoped to publish them as a companion to *The Cross of Job* (1916), *The Cross of Jeremiah* (1925), and *The Cross of the Servant* (1926), little books widely treasured for their deep religious insight and sympathy. A first draft of "The Marriage of Hosea" appeared in the *Baptist Quarterly*, Vol. V (1931), pp. 204 f. The lectures on Ezekiel were prepared for the Vacation Term of Biblical Study at Oxford in 1943, and, when he delivered them, Dr. Robinson was already suffering the first effects of the illness from which he passed away in 1945. It will be found that there are a number of illuminating contacts between the two sets of lectures.

I am indebted to Professor H. H. Rowley for his kindness in reading the typescript and lending the authority of his judgment to my own belief that these lectures should be printed, even though they cannot now have Dr. Robinson's own final revision. I have made only such editorial corrections and additions as seemed essential. My colleague, the Rev. L. H. Brockington, has kindly assisted me with the proofs.

ERNEST A. PAYNE.

Regent's Park College,
Oxford.

Contents

7

The Cross of Hosea

THE MARRIAGE OF HOSEA

The chief thing that Bacon had to say about love was that "it troubleth men's fortunes"; and about marriage: "He that hath Wife and Children hath given Hostages to Fortune." Had he thought with understanding of the prophet Hosea he might have enlarged his horizon towards that of another famous essayist. Emerson, writing on *Compensation*, adds the necessary complement concerning the gain that may lie in a man's apparent loss. "Whilst he sits on the cushion of advantages, he goes to sleep. When he is pushed, tormented, defeated, he has a chance to learn something." The sorrows of Hosea were his "chance of the prize of learning love".

How love might be, hath been indeed, and is;

so that his "soul's prowess" came to lie in his faithful answer to "life's proof":

Does God love,
And will ye hold that truth against the world?

Yet, as Emerson so emphatically asserts, this law of reciprocity does not work mechanically in the spiritual realm; it is the evil to which we do not succumb that is a benefactor. True as that is of our common humanity, it is especially true of a prophet, and of such a prophet as Hosea, whose call lay in his experience, and whose experience was made by his own attitude to the events which befell him. Even in that ancient world, so remote from our modernity, his theology was "the theology of experience".

The modern interest in the psychology of religious experience, combined with critical study of the records of Hebrew prophets, has led to a great deal of attention being given to their inner life and thought. This is well worth while, both for exegesis and for theology in general, though the lack of information about their outer life and circumstances usually leaves our results somewhat uncertain in detail. Their lives were so subordinated to their messages that it is often only through those messages that we can reconstruct their lives. This fact makes the story of Hosea's marriage the more important, for here, if anywhere, we may see the outer event shaping the inner experience, and its resultant expression in the prophet's "Thus saith the Lord".

The account of the marriage of Hosea is contained in the first and the third chapters of the collection of oracles bearing his name. According to the first chapter, Hosea is commanded to take a harlot for his wife, and children of harlotry; he accordingly marries Gomer bath Diblaim, who subsequently has three children, to whom the prophet gives symbolic names, which become the texts of prophetic messages concerning Israel. According to the third chapter, Hosea is commanded to love an unnamed woman, loved by a paramour, and an adulteress. He obeys by purchasing her, apparently from some kind of undescribed servitude, and by setting her apart for what seems to be a probationary period. These are practically all our facts, and anything else is an interpretation of them, justified or unjustifiable.

1. *The Actual Events*

The first point we have to decide is this—did these events actually happen, or are they an allegory by which the unfaithfulness of Israel to Yahweh might be the more vividly set forth? I have no hesitation at all in regarding them as real events, issuing from the sex-relation of man and woman, though the two chapters mingle interpretation with event in what to us is a somewhat confusing way. It is not necessary to suppose that Hosea married a woman whom he knew at the time to be unchaste. The terms of the narrative may simply mean that when the prophet did interpret his own life prophetically in the light of after events as being under the providential guidance of God, he saw that he had, in fact, though unconsciously at the time, taken to himself a woman *destined* to be a wife of harlotry and to bear children of harlotry. This seems more likely than that the prophet knowingly married a woman of unchaste spirit or conduct, though such a supposition could not in itself be excluded as impossible. The symbolical acts of the Hebrew prophets, such as Isaiah's walking about Jerusalem for three years in the dress of a captive-slave, are often strange to us, and are explicable only by the completeness of surrender to the prophetic impulse. But it is more natural to suppose that a discovery of Gomer's infidelity was made subsequently, and that the story of the first chapter has been written down (not necessarily by the prophet himself) from this subsequent standpoint. We have a parallel to this prophetic interpretation of an actual event which happened independently of it, in the symbolic meaning which Ezekiel gives to his wife's death (Ezek. 24: 15 ff.), when he abstains from the usual mourning customs to symbolize the effect of the fall of Jerusalem upon the people. We have another example in Jeremiah's purchase of family property at Anathoth, of which the symbolic significance emerges only after the event (32: 7). In further support of the view that Hosea's marriage was an actual event allegorically interpreted, and not an invented allegory, we may notice such details as the name of Gomer, and the weaning of her daughter, or the details about the purchase-price of

13

the unnamed woman in the third chapter, which have no significance for allegory at all.

A more difficult question to decide concerns the relation of the third chapter to the first. Is it sequel, parallel, or prelude? The prevalent, and the *prima facie* natural view, is that the third chapter is the sequel to the first, the intervening chapter making the allegorical application of the first. According to this view, the unnamed woman of the third chapter is still Gomer of the first. But in the interval, she must be supposed to have left her husband and to have passed into other hands—those of a private owner, or possibly of a temple, at which she may be serving as one of the "religious" prostitutes of the time. We are not told directly of this separation, at least in the present records of Hosea's life and ministry, any more than we are told what actually happened after the period of probation. But we are given to understand that Hosea intends to take Gomer back to his home when she is ready for it. The second view—that the third chapter is parallel to the first—is based chiefly on the arguments that the important fact of Gomer's departure from her husband ought not to be left to the imagination; that Gomer would have been definitely named or indicated, if this were a sequel; and that the narrative of the third chapter is in the first person, i.e. autobiographic, whilst that of the first is in the third person, i.e. biographic, a fact which is taken to suggest that they come from different hands, describing in different ways the prophet's one and only marriage. The third view, that Chapter 3 gives us Hosea's own account of events *preceding* his marriage, has been more recently advocated. According to this, Hosea knowingly married a woman of unchaste character, who was openly living with a paramour, but did this only after a period of probation. He tells us this in the third chapter, written at a time when the marriage had not taken place, and the children

14

of the first chapter accordingly had not yet been born. We are informed of these subsequent events by a later biographer, and may infer that the adultery of Gomer took place after the birth of the first child. It is alleged that we have no further knowledge of Hosea's marriage experience than is given in Chapter 1, and therefore no ground in it for ascribing optimistic prophecies to the prophet, as his final word. The hopeful period came earlier in his life, whilst he still thought that Gomer might be successfully redeemed from sin.

Obviously, the more romantic story is that of the first view—that Hosea seeks to reclaim the fallen Gomer at the end, and not at the beginning. But we must not allow the attraction of this "romance", or its greater theological suggestiveness, to sway our exegesis. Our first duty is to decide, on grounds of literary criticism, which is the more probable view, and only then to test this by its larger relations. Of the three views, the third seems to me least probable and most arbitrary, and it involves emendation of the text in the interests of a theory. It throws the emphasis of the prophet on the reclamation of a woman who has not been faithless to *him*, instead of on that of a faithless wife who has borne at least one child of which he is the father. It presupposes a double unchastity, and confuses the allegorical application. The second view, that the difference of the narratives is due to their being by different hands, and that they give an inside and outside account of the same events, is difficult to maintain, because the events are not the same. In the first chapter Hosea is bidden to take an unchaste woman, in the third to love an adulterous woman. In the first, the births of three children are described in succession, in a way that implies the passage of at least five years; in the third, a woman is bought for a slave's price, and put into isolation for "many days". The two narratives seem irreconcilable, if they are to be regarded as parallel accounts of Hosea's marriage. Certainly, no one would be likely to refer them to the same set of incidents, unless as an escape from greater difficulties. But it is hard to see why we should not take Chapters 1 and 3 in their present order as parts of a prophetical narrative referring to different periods of Hosea's life. They may not both be written by the prophet; indeed, the change of person from the third to the first suggests this; and it is more natural to regard the first chapter as giving a report by a biographer, which more or less faithfully reflects the earlier life of Hosea; whilst, in the third chapter, we have a fragment of later autobiography from the prophet himself. There are many parallels in the prophetical books, e.g. in Jeremiah, to this interchange of biography and autobiography. The fact that Gomer is not named in the third chapter means nothing if "a woman beloved of her paramour and an adulteress" is a sufficient characterization of her, as it would be if she had been unfaithful to Hosea in the course of their married life. It is true that we have to infer this fact from the first description of her, as "a wife of harlotry"; but this applies to all other theories which seek a basis for the allegory in real events. We have always to remember the allusive character of such writing; no more is named than the writer or speaker requires at the moment. We should not have heard that Ezekiel was married, had he not been led to make his wife's funeral a symbol of the national tragedy.

In the present arrangement of the first three chapters there is an intelligible order. We have, first, the marriage followed by the births of three children, with the suggestion of their mother's infidelity to her husband. We have, in the second chapter, the allegorical application of these events: "Plead with your mother, plead; for she is not my wife, neither am I her husband," says Yahweh to the people of the land, i.e. its children, who are "children of harlotry" (2: 2 ff.). This condemnation passes into the promise of a new betrothal of Israel to Yahweh, with new and permanent qualities, and a reversal of the old condemnatory names of the children. This latter part of the chapter obviously runs into the ground of the real experience of the prophet in the following chapter; his love persists, in spite of the infidelity, and is interpreted as divine command to win back his faithless wife to better ways. The experiential text of the sermon found in the second chapter therefore lies in the first and third chapters, taken in this sequence; but the preacher reserves the closing part of his text till the sermon is concluded, when it becomes a human illustration of the divine truth. There are difficulties enough in the oracles of Hosea without exaggerating those of the opening chapters. We may, therefore, remain content with the ordinary view of the events of Hosea's marriage, with which many Old Testament scholars are still satisfied; the chief fault to find with it seems to be that it has lost the charm of novelty. On the other hand, if sound in itself, it does supply a ground for regarding Hosea as not finally a pessimist as to his nation, and for ascribing to him the oracles which are promises, as well as those which are warnings, and condemnations.

2. *The Application to Religion*

The justification for this discussion of Hosea's marriage is that it has important results not only for exegesis, but also for theology. In regard to exegesis, a careful study of the book of Hosea would show how deeply the oracles which it contains are coloured by the experience of his marriage; how frequently the figure of marital infidelity enters into them; how warm is the feeling with which the relation of Yahweh to Israel is described; how passionate is the longing of God portrayed in them to betroth a faithful people to Himself. We may not feel warranted in relating all the oracles to this one series of events as closely and comprehensively as some have done; but there can be little doubt that the chief psychological explanation of the oracles is derived from Hosea's relations with Gomer. It may even be that the bitterness of the prophet's attack on the immorality of the high places and of the priests connected with them is due to a personal element—that it was from one of these sanctuaries that he had, in the literal sense, to redeem the temple-prostitute Gomer, because she had first been led astray by the licensed sexuality of their festivals, and had left her husband for professional connection with a sanctuary.

There is certainly a depth of personal emotion in this book which can be paralleled nowhere else save in the greater prophet so like Hosea—Jeremiah—who knew the sorrows of a lonely and threatened life, as Hosea did those of an unhappy marriage. But our present concern is not with the detailed exegesis of the book of Hosea, but with its theological significance. He is the first to make a profoundly ethical application of the figure of marriage to the relation between God and man. Of course, the sex element had taken a great place in primitive religion, including the Canaanite. The mystery of sex, like the mystery of blood, was an inevitable feature in early interpretation of the comprehensive mystery of life, and of its relation to the superhuman powers surrounding man and his existence. The conception of the God as physically married to the land and as producing its fruits seems part of the idea underlying the fertility cults (cf. 1: 2). But the moral side of the sex relation, the higher principles which lead to its sublimation in human experience, and may make human love the most divine of all man's experiences, because the most fully reflecting the love of God, and preparing man to understand and

18

respond to it—all this great line of thought which culminates in the Gospel of the New Testament was initiated by Hosea. We see it already working in the Jewish interpretation of the Song of Songs as an allegory of the history of Israel, the bride of Yahweh, from the Exodus to the final restoration of all things. An anthology of love lyrics, containing nothing that is religious at all in the ordinary sense, was thus raised to what a Jewish Rabbi called the Holy of Holies of Israel's sacred literature. We know how profoundly the figure has affected Christian thought and its devotional vocabulary, from Saint Paul's comparison of marriage with the relation of Christ and the Church onwards. Hosea is the first begetter of all this line of thought, and he holds this place because of the actual experiences of his life, prophetically interpreted.

We have here, then, a supreme example of the place of experience in the prophetic consciousness, and of the warp of human life on the loom of Scripture, across which the shuttle of the Spirit of God so constantly moved. We are reminded here, at the beginning of Israel's higher conceptions of God that revelation lies in and through that unity of religious experience in which the human and the divine personality lose their "otherness". In the prophetic consciousness, which is one of the noblest kinds of religious consciousness, all is human, and all is divine. These things have been made familiar to us by historical criticism of the Bible, but it cannot be said that their full theological consequences for a doctrine of revelation have yet been recognized.

A sound doctrine of revelation really raises the issues of the Incarnation itself—the fundamental kinship of human and divine personality. So long as revelation is regarded as the communication to man of a truth about God already existing externally to the man himself, *in that form*, so long the process remains mechanical; and reduces man to a mere amanuensis, as Calvin indeed held. But when we see that the revelation is made in and through a human experience, in which experience the truth to be revealed is first created, *in that form*, we are ready to face the implication of this, viz. that human experience *is* capable of representing the divine. There will of course be all kinds of limitation due to man's imperfection, mental and moral, and we must suppose a divine *kenosis* in God's acceptance of these limitations for His purpose—a *kenosis* as real in its way as that described by the apostle Paul in regard to the Eternal Son of God. But if the love of Hosea for his faithless wife does really represent, in spite of its human limitations, the love of God for Israel; if the word "love", in fact, is to be allowed any human connotation at all in regard to God, it must be because the human personality is in some sense akin to the divine (cf. 11: 4) though far below it (11: 9). Moreover, the revelation is made through the unity of fellowship between God and man and is born of their intercourse.

The prophets doubtless interpreted the message as coming from without, in accord with their general psychology. They saw visions of external happenings; heard voices, as with their physical ears; felt the hand of Yahweh upon them in quasi-physical compulsions. But all these features belong to their own interpretation of the psychical events, and we may describe them in different terms without injustice to the events themselves or their divine significance as "revelation". The sorrowful experience of Hosea as a man and not as a prophet, might have had no such significance, however warm his affection for Gomer, and however loyal his endeavour to raise her from shame. The new fact is made when Hosea, the prophet, reinterprets this experience as having such significance, and makes the prophetic "venture of faith" in saying that this is how God sorrows and God loves. He could not make this venture unless he implicitly believed that God's nature was somehow like his own. No doubt he does not explicitly put it like this; in fact, he represents Yahweh as saying: "I am God and not man." The transcendence of God is explicit; the immanence of God is implicit. But the whole revelation through prophecy rests on the assumption that human experience and thought *can* reveal God, which means that there is no fundamental unlikeness between the human and the divine personality.

3. *The Higher Anthropomorphism*

This assumption, which we may call "the higher anthropomorphism", has its negative side in the prophetic attitude towards idolatry, first revealed in Hosea himself (8: 4 ff.). Just as they felt that the inner consciousness of man and his outer experience in history could and did reveal God, so they felt that the material representation of Him in wood and metal and stone could not reveal Him. The human medium of revelation was not only infinitely higher, but was itself dynamic and ever moving onwards, so as to be capable of becoming more and more adequate to the unveiling of the living God. The material medium was not only incomparably inferior to the human consciousness, since it was the mere semblance of lifeless flesh, but it was once and for all time fixed and static. Carry forward these two lines of revelation—the spiritual and the material—and you come logically to the contrast between the revelation in the prophet of Nazareth, and that in the Torah, supposed to have been given in its perfection and all-sufficiency by Moses, which imprisons the revelation of God in the letter of the Law. The religion of the Incarnation continues the religion of the prophets, not only in moral and religious teaching, but also in implicit theology. The prophetic emphasis on the human conscience as the most adequate revelation of God is the true forerunner and anticipation of the Prologue to the Fourth Gospel: "the law was given by Moses; grace and truth came by Jesus Christ".

4. *The Passibility of God*

This leads to the question of the doctrine of the passibility of God, the ascription of sorrow and suffering to Him. Dr. J. K. Mozley, in *The Impassibility of God* (1926), has virtually confined himself to an historical record, pointing out the marked contrast between ancient and modern Christian thought on this subject. Until the Reformation, and indeed after it, there was "a steady and continuous, if not quite unbroken, tradition in Christian theology as to the freedom of the divine nature from all suffering and from any potentiality of suffering" (p. 127). In modern theology, on the other hand, there has been a strong reaction against the doctrine of impassibility, represented by such theologians as Bushnell, Fairbairn, Canon Streeter and Bishop Temple; and by such Christian philosophers as Lotze and Pringle-Pattison. The last-named claims that the open secret of the Universe is: "a God who lives in the perpetual giving of Himself, who shares in the life of His finite creatures, bearing in them and with them the whole burden of their finitude, their sinful wanderings and sorrows, and the suffering without which they cannot be made perfect" (*The Idea of God*, p. 411). Professor H. R. Mackintosh says, in *The Christian Experience of Forgiveness* (p. 216): "Ideas of the Divine impassibility derived from ages which were very far from humane, and which too often regarded suffering unconcernedly as a mark of the weak and the vanquished, can now make little appeal." On the other hand, we have such a study as the late Baron von Hügel's *Suffering and God*, published in the second series of his *Essays*, in which he contends that whilst men sin and suffer, and Christ suffers but does not sin, there is as little room for suffering as for sin in God, who is pure Joy. This essay seems to me quite wrong in its contention that the prophets of Israel did not attribute suffering to God (p. 186), and that what they say is to be dismissed as imagery. Let us apply that contention to one of the most moving passages in the Book of Hosea (11: 8, 9):

> *How shall I give thee up, Ephraim?*
> *How shall I hand thee over, Israel?*
> *How shall I give thee up as Admah, set thee as Zeboim?*
> *My heart is turned upon me,*
> *My compassions are kindled together;*
> *I will not carry out my hot anger,*
> *I will not again destroy Ephraim.*

If we say that this expresses only a passionless "sympathy", and that God does not sorrow and does not suffer because of the sin of His people, how much force is left in such words? How can a God who is *apathetic* be also *sympathetic*? But if Hosea's words are interpreted by that experience of the prophet in which they seem to have arisen—Hosea's own inability to detach himself from Gomer because of his sorrowing and suffering love for her, then the words become charged with a Gospel, and point on directly to the truths of the New Testament. We may indeed ask how there can be "sympathy" at all without suffering? If sympathy be a "feeling with" the sufferer, is not that very feeling itself a form of suffering? If the love of God is more than a metaphor, must not the suffering of God be as real, though with all the qualifications in both love and suffering which come from the reference to God instead of man. It seems a dangerous thing to dismiss such sayings as imagery, unless we go on to admit quite frankly that all human language about God is but symbolic, though not the less capable of symbolizing ultimate truths. The danger is continued in the realm of Christology, when with von Hügel and many others we say that Christ suffered as man, but not as God. Somehow that distinction, however convenient to the theologian, does not seem to ring true to the story of the Gospels, or to the strong language of the Epistle to the Hebrews about the suffering of the Son of God.

The final joy of God must be beyond question; the Christian conception of God cannot be of a worn and anxious and burdened traveller, fearful lest he may not reach his world-goal. God is a burden-bearer, according to the Hebrew prophets (Isaiah 46: 3, 4), but it is because He carries *willingly* the burden of His people. He is, as a later Jewish teacher said, "forever young", and His triumph is no uncertain thing in a universe of risks. But the Christian conception seems to be that of a triumph through the Cross, a victory through apparent defeat, a joy that is all the richer joy because it is won, like that of Jesus, through great suffering, voluntarily accepted and endured for the joy that was set before Him. The conception of a God who cannot suffer makes theology much more manageable, but leaves it high and dry, like the gods of the Epicureans:

> . . . *who haunt*
> *The lucid interspace of world and world,*
> *Where never creeps a cloud, or moves a wind,*
> *Nor ever falls the least white star of snow,*
> *Nor ever lowest roll of thunder moans,*
> *Nor sound of human sorrow mounts to mar*
> *Their sacred everlasting calm!*

5. The Relation to Historical Revelation

Finally, it is in place to notice here the relation of such

an experience as Hosea's to the whole validity of an historical revelation; that is, the adequacy of a revelation of the infinite God in and through finite events. Both Judaism and Christianity are committed to such events; eliminate the Exodus and Sinai, eliminate the Cross and the Resurrection, and you change the very essence of both religions, and their faith that God is ever active and that He is known by what He does in history. What do we lose when we play with the idea that we may retain the ideas of the Gospel and not concern ourselves with the question as to what actually happened in history? I cannot express it better than Dr. H. G. Wood has done, in his book, *Christianity and the Nature of History*: "While all the ideal values may remain if you impugn the historic record set forth in the gospels, these ideal values are not certified to the common man as inherent in the very nature of things" (p. 28). It is that note of actuality which is common to the whole revelation in the Bible, and to a prophetic experience such as Hosea's in particular. It was one thing to hold in general that God loved Israel; it was another to have that confirmed by the analogy of his own experience, and to know that God *so* loved Israel, as Hosea found himself loving Gomer. The experience both confirmed the idea and enlightened it, by bringing a new standard of measurement to its appreciation. The love of God could not be less than the love of man, so the love of man became a pledge and a revelation of the love of God.

THE INWARDNESS OF SIN

The characteristic of God is grace; the characteristic of man in his present stage of development is sin, the production of which is the proof of his highest attribute, that is, his freedom to act even in rebellion against God. Now it is one of the tendencies of modern preaching, as of modern hearing, to take God's grace for granted as something that is self-evident and to dismiss any emphasis on man's sin as rather in the nature of a theological fiction. This attitude altogether ignores the fact that all of us know a great deal about sin from our direct experience, whereas we know the grace of God only at the circumference of His being where it touches our life. It is quite true that sin is a theological term and that it denotes the religious aspect of moral evil. In the strict sense of the word, there can be no sin where there is no religion, but the substance and content of sin, that is, moral evil, belong to the undeniable experience of all of us, and all of us know a great deal about it, far more in fact than we know about God's grace. When we turn to the masterpieces of literature, it will not be long before we are faced with some adequate recognition of this truth as a rebuke to our superficial neglect of it. Let us take, for example, one of the great studies of sin which Shakespeare has given us, viz. *Macbeth*, and see if it does not reveal certain permanent and universal characteristics of moral evil, whether we call it sin or not.

In the first place, a study of *Macbeth* can teach us that sin is that which it does. We see the evil of it in its consequences, both within and without; in the surrender of a nature capable of great things to the power of superstition, to the denial of all honour and loyalty, to deed after deed of cruelty and wrong, till the sinner is left alone and helpless, hating the very life that he has made for himself.

In the second place, sin, like righteousness, is nurtured socially. It would often shrink with horror from itself as it begins to see its own consequences, if it were not for the spur and encouragement of other sinners. Evil, like good, needs the momentum of other lives to be added to itself in order to achieve its full power and reveal its true nature. Macbeth, without his wife, would never have done his first deed of evil. On the other hand, Banquo's fellowship might have saved him from it. But the heart gathers its own society and by the momentum of that society becomes capable of the worst.

In the third place, however close this dependence of sin on social environment and fellowship, sin begins within, long before that outer occasion and opportunity which is often called temptation. It begins, in the case of Macbeth, in the unbridled ambition, the lust for self-glory, the dwelling on the thought of selfish ends, till evil aims are designed to gratify the lust and the heart is ready for its external opportunity. This emphasis on the inwardness of sin which is so conspicuous in Shakespeare's study of Macbeth is in no degree cancelled by his recognition of the weird sisters as a point of contact with the supernatural world. They are, after all, merely an extension of Macbeth's social environment, a supernatural parallel to Lady Macbeth herself, in the natural order, and their presence and action do not in the least exonerate Macbeth. They do not lead Banquo astray.

In the fourth place, sin is shown to be doomed by its intrinsic character. It creates its own penalties, alienating the good which might have brought deliverance from it, hardening itself to worse and worse deeds which dispense with even the poor excuse of its own beginning. Sooner or later, it finds the universe arrayed against it; for sin is the challenge to the whole of things by the individual man, which is the sheerest and uttermost folly. Sin ends by destroying the sinner. Granville Barker rightly sees this in Macbeth and his wife (*A Companion to Shakespeare Studies*, pp. 79, 82): "the ebbing of life within these two, their death while they still live, for here is the essential tragedy . . . in the sleep-walking scene we see her already spiritually dead . . . the man's living spirit does seem at last to shrivel to a cipher . . . he too is dead before he dies."

The student of Macbeth will find all these things set out in the concrete terms of human character and destiny without any suggestion of theology. They recur in the study of every human life, in greater or less degree, though entangled with the veils and disguises of the daily routine which it is the dramatist's business to strip off. Certainly they may be found by the student of the Book of Hosea; in our study of the theology of sin as here represented, we shall find the same four aspects of sin presented not less definitely even if in obscurer terms, because of the remoter vehicle of expression, i.e. that sin is what it does, that it is socially nurtured, that it begins within, and that it is self-destructive.

1. *Hosea's Personal Experience of Moral Evil*

It was Hosea's personal experience of moral evil in Gomer, his wife, that gave him, at the cost of so much suffering, such insight into the nature and activity of sin. Thornton Wilder in his little play, *The Angel that Troubled the Waters*, gives the plea of one who seeks for healing in vain, saying: "It is no shame to boast to an Angel of what I might still do in Love's service were I freed from his bondage." To this the Angel's reply is:

"Without your wound, where would your power be? The very angels themselves cannot persuade the wretched and blundering children on earth as can one human being broken in the wheels of living." Hosea's power was in his wound. He saw that sin spoilt life, both in its quality and in its relations. By his intimate knowledge of what Gomer's infidelity meant to himself, he entered into a new sympathy with the God who is made to suffer through the sin of man. If it be true that moral evil concerns God, and because He is a holy God involves Him in suffering [according to our argument in the discussion of Hosea's marriage] then it is only by our own reaction to the sin of others in holy love that we can understand God's consciousness in that small degree which is possible for man at all.

We may say indeed that only the holy man, in proportion to the degree of his holiness, knows what sin is. This sounds a paradox, yet only because we have such artificial conceptions of what holiness is. If we define it by the Christian standards, which means if we measure it by the holiness of Christ, then its chief and essential attribute is love, and love that inevitably suffers through every contact with moral evil. It suffered the more because it cannot disown its own responsibility for the redemption of the sinner. The last thing that holy love is capable of doing is to stand on one side, saying: "I am holier than thou, and thou in thy sin art no concern of mine." It is this false conception of holiness, this negative idea of freedom from pollution, rather than the positive idea of burden-bearing, which makes it difficult for us to realize the true nature of holiness, and, therefore, the true nature of sin. Life contains many realities which can be known only through actual contact with them, or participation in them. It is one thing to treat them speculatively. It is quite another to handle them in real life.

Just as Job was brought from his suffering to an inner knowledge of the truth of innocence and the falsity of contemporary theological theory, so was Hosea, through his unhappy association with Gomer, trained and schooled in the university of life to graduate with such high honours in the knowledge of God and of man. Hosea saw what sin meant when he looked on Gomer corrupted by its vice and entangled in its toils. He imagined further what the sin of Israel must mean to God, and his faith in God's final victory over the evil spirit of Israel was the reflection of his own assurance that his love would conquer the spirit of infidelity in Gomer and win her back to a new betrothal, holy and righteous. His enlightened eyes looked forth from his home to the wider horizon. The moral and religious evils of his day had, for him, thenceforward a new significance. He saw that they sprang from the inner spirit of whoredom, which he had known at close quarters and could now recognize on the larger scale (4: 12; 5: 4). He saw how this moral evil was rooted in social relations, buttressed and defended by the vested interests of kings and princes, priests and prophets, passed on from one generation to another in continuous social solidarity. He saw, too, that its end was death, except for one divine possibility: that which Browning puts into the mouth of the Pope in *The Ring and the Book* when he conceives that even the arch-villain, Guido, might have the true nature of things revealed to him by some sudden blaze of light, as he himself had once seen Naples by a lightning flash. The difference is, however, that Hosea's hope is not like that of most of the prophets, based on catastrophic and eschatological expectations. He believes, rather, that a patient and enduring love, eloquent through its suffering, will at last avail to penetrate to the spirit within and transform its alienation. Is not Guido's last cry itself an appeal to his own so deeply wronged wife:

"Pompilia, will you let them murder me?" Hosea's aspiration and his expectation are, for the Christian, the prophecy of that which should be in the fullness of the time.

2. The Social Environment of Sin

If we are to see Israel's sin as it met the eyes of Hosea, we must first reconstruct, in imagination, the general background of economic, social and religious life in those days. We must think of the people generally as living in small towns and villages, their one-roomed houses usually clustered on the slopes of one of the hills of Ephraim. Below would be the village well, to which the women would come morning and evening; at the gate, or in some adjacent spot, the men would meet when they had common business; above the houses, on the hill-top, would be the "high place", the local sanctuary. The majority of the people would be engaged in agricultural work, though by this time some were beginning Israel's future world-career of trading, under the guidance of the Canaanites. On the hill-side there would be the grapes and olives to tend, and the rock-presses in which to trample out their juices; down in the valley grew the wheat and barley, which would have to be carried in due season to the threshing-floor, up beside the "high place" near the hill-top. In the little houses, the oil and the meal would be kept in earthen jars, and supplemented by various fruits; flesh would be eaten only on festival days. Their clothing was of the simplest—a close-fitting tunic, and an outer cloak, used as a sleeping-cover.

The social organization of these village-groups was hardly more elaborate than their manner of life. It centred in the family group, over which the father ruled; and in the local assembly of male citizens, under the leadership of the elders. The methods of the wandering desert tribe were largely retained in this simple village community, where all men knew each other's affairs. The king counted for little, except in time of war, or when his agents collected some tax or other. The priest at the high place was much more important, for he could give oracles or advice on practical difficulties; the prophet was a more irregular and occasional factor. The community was controlled by customs, local and national, rather than by formal codes of law; these customs would have to be applied to particular circumstances by the sense of the community, interpreted by the elders. The local assembly was at once judicial, military and religious; a citizen might be called upon to act in any one of these three capacities, at any time. The religious life of the town or village centred in the "high place". There would be found the altar, developed from its primitive form of a rough block of unhewn stone, and, near it, perhaps, some ancient and sacred tree; at any rate, there would be the Ashera, a wooden post, and the Mazzebah, a stone pillar, these being survivals of more primitive tree- and stone-worship. In some cases, there was also the image of Yahweh, the ox being the favourite symbol for Him amongst an agricultural people, because of its strength. To this high place the people of the district, men and women, would flock at the time of the great agricultural festivals, and to a less degree at new moons and sabbaths; whilst many private visits would be made to the sanctuary by those who brought some gift and wanted some favour. If an animal sacrifice was offered the oldest method was to drain, on the altar, its blood, as belonging to the deity, whilst the family and their friends feasted on the flesh, and so realized communion with their god.

These, then, are the main outlines of life in the northern kingdom down to the eighth century. It is easy to see some of the abuses and perils of such a free and un-systematized social life, especially when the influx of new wealth disturbed the former social relationships. In the first place, luxury and extravagance replaced the older simplicity—houses of hewn stone; furniture of ivory; cushions of silk; costly and elaborate dress; the drinking of wine from bowls; the eating of flesh every day; drunkenness and gluttony. The rich turned from the good old simple ways of nomad life, which the Puritan Rechabites maintained for centuries. In the second place, the administration of justice pressed hardly on such as were not represented in the local community. Women who were wives or daughters would be pro-tected by their fathers and husbands; but the woman who was a widow would have no one naturally bound to speak for her; and the orphan and the alien would be in like condition. The wealthier would acquire influence in many ways, and even-handed justice would be harder to get, especially because of the bribery of the judges, in which the wealthier could outbid his fellows. It was a hard thing to be poor in Israel in those days; you might be forced to sell not only your land-holding, but your-self as well, into slavery, to get food for your family in some time of famine. In this way the smaller holdings were being absorbed into larger estates, sometimes through sheer economic pressure; at others, perhaps, through such "methods of barbarism" as Ahab had practised on Naboth. Then, in the third place, the con-ditions of religion were lamentable. The modes of wor-ship at the high places had been taken over from the Canaanites, with all their furniture, and all their cus-toms. The god of each locality had been called its Baal, or "lord", whom the Canaanites had worshipped as the giver of all the fertility of the district. These various Baalim were honoured through what would be reckoned by us the grossest sexual immorality. When Israel dis-

33

possessed the Canaanites, it meant that Yahweh was dispossessing their Baalim. What was more natural, then, than that He should become heir to their worship, and be worshipped Himself as the local Baal, when His people settled down to agricultural life, and needed a God of agriculture? In this way, then, the older religion of Yahweh was passing out of recognition, and was being transformed from the crude but moral religion of the desert to a more cultured but non-moral, even immoral, nature-worship. Against this triple deterioration, then, the growing luxury, the evident injustice, the flagrant immorality of religion, the prophets Amos and Hosea become the protesting voice of Yahweh Himself.

There are, however, certain features of this prophetic condemnation peculiar to Hosea, and with these we are especially concerned. His emphasis falls, much more than that of Amos, on the actual immorality of the cult and of its priests, and he seems to be the first to denounce the idolatry which formed part of the worship of Yahweh. The detached oracles begin (4–5: 7) with the denunciation of the priests. *They* are primarily responsible for the ignorance displayed by the people; they feed on the sin of Israel, since they profit by the sacrificial offerings and their multiplication; they have fallen to the level of the people themselves—"like people, like priest". They are even accused of using the sanctuaries as their base of operations for actual robbery and murder (6: 9). The fatal attraction of the cult practised at the sanctuaries is compared with the hunter's snare and net and pit. No wonder that there is actual whoredom and adultery amongst the people where such evil things are consecrated as a part of the ritual (4: 13, 14; the reference is to the fertility rites of Baalism). The bull-images of the sanctuaries are denounced again and again (2: 8 RVm; 4: 17; 8: 4–6; 9: 6; 10: 5, 10; 11: 2; 13: 2; 14: 3,

34

8); the term "calf" is purposely contemptuous for the small bull-images of wood or baser metal plated with silver or gold. These represented the God of Israel as the source of the fertility of the land, as some of them had probably represented the local Baalim, before they were transferred to the cult of Yahweh.

Further, Hosea is the pioneer of a new attitude towards the monarchy. According to the earlier of the two stories of its inception in the First Book of Samuel (9; 10: 1–16; 11: 1–11, 15) the first king was chosen and anointed by Samuel, acting with the full approval and by the inspiration of Yahweh. But the kingship was bound up with the patronage of the cult which the eighth-century prophets had been led to condemn. The rebellion of Jehu against the dynasty of Omri a century earlier had been instigated by the prophets Elijah and Elisha and supported by the founder of the Puritan Rechabites. But the cruel and reckless bloodshed of Jehu's rebellion revolted Hosea as much as the religious practices of the dynasty against which Jehu rebelled; this is the meaning of the words "I will visit the blood of Jezreel upon the house of Jehu" (1: 4.). Hosea's lot was cast in an unsettled age when the kings of Israel had little to commend them; after the death of Jeroboam II in 743, there were six kings in twenty-eight years, only one of whom died a natural death, so full was the time of plots and counterplots and assassinations. Altogether, Hosea is brought to a point at which the monarchy seems an evil thing in itself, and an abandonment of Yahweh. That attitude is reflected in the later story of the origin of the kingship (found in 1 Sam. 8; 10: 17–24; 11: 12–15), which represents it as a defection from Yahweh from the very beginning when it was condemned by Samuel. The origin of that quite inconsistent story seems to be Hosea's similar view of the monarchy, in the light of what it had come to mean for Israel. So he announces judgment on the royal house (5: 1), a party to contemporary evils (7: 3, 5; 9: 15) as well as the victim of them (7: 7, 10: 7). His attitude is explicitly stated in the words "They have set up kings, but not by me; they have made princes, and I knew it not" (8: 4). . . . "I gave thee kings in my anger and took them away in my wrath" (13: 11; collective).

Besides all this, Hosea denounces those foreign relations which were so characteristic of the politics of the times. Israel lay between Assyria and Egypt, the plaything of both. Against the menace of Assyria, the only external refuge was Egypt. So there was a pro-Assyrian and a pro-Egyptian party, and between them the history of those days runs its troublous course. "Ephraim, he mixeth himself among the peoples: Ephraim is a half-baked cake" (7: 8) or "a silly dove" (7: 11); "they call unto Egypt, they go to Assyria". To Hosea, as to his contemporary in the south, Isaiah, the only true policy was no policy at all, but a penitent return to Yahweh, whose business it was to look after His recovered bride (2: 19 f.).

Such were the chief social and religious institutions of the time which the prophet condemned. They were to him the entrenchments of moral evil, at once expressing and reinforcing the "spirit of whoredom", the inner spirit of alienation from Yahweh, which he recognized as the real root of all the trouble, in the national as in the domestic tragedy of his experience.

3. *The Inner Alienation*

Hosea's phrase to describe the inner source of this externally visible alienation from God is "the spirit of whoredom".[1] It is obviously drawn from his own

[1] Cf. the spirit of perverseness (Isa. 19: 14); of uncleanness (Zech. 13: 2); and of jealousy (Num. 5: 14).

experience of Gomer's conduct, and denotes the actual impulse to sexual immorality which was at the root of her infidelity. In its figurative transference to Israel, it denotes the inner spirit which found outer expression in all the acts which Hosea has been seen to condemn. This is evident from the context of the two passages in which Hosea employs the phrase. In 4: 12 he says that the spirit of whoredom has caused the people to wander away[1] from the true God, and he illustrates this by reference to divination by means of the sacred tree or the sacred staff, and to the sacrifice and incense-offering upon the high places, with which sacred prostitution was connected, and also to the idolatry to which Ephraim was wedded (17). All this was done in the name of Yahweh, but the prophet contends that it springs from a false conception of His nature and requirements; it is the lower passions of men which produce this actual immorality and this religious infidelity. In the second context (5: 4), the phrase is in parallelism with the words "they know not Yahweh". It is the opposite of the promise in 2: 20, where the outcome of the new betrothal in righteousness, and in justice, in loving-kindness and in mercies, is so described. To know Yahweh is to be just and loving; not to know Him is to be the opposite, and this injustice and disloyalty spring from within. They seek God zealously, but do not find Him, because they have this false idea of what He is and what He wants; He has withdrawn Himself from such a false approach to Him, and their very deeds themselves will forever prevent a true approach (5: 6).

This conception of sin as essentially consisting in an inner spirit which manifests itself in outer acts was something new in the history of religion, however familiar and obvious it has become to us. There is nothing in Amos, the immediate predecessor of Hosea, which

[1] Like a lost animal (Exod. 23: 4) or a drunken man (Isa. 28: 7).

37

goes as deep as this. The prophets generally gave a new moral content to sin, in place of the older idea of a broken taboo, and infringement of a non-moral "holiness". But it was Hosea who penetrated to the genuinely religious aspect of sin, as consisting in an alienated spirit. In this he is notably followed by Jeremiah, his spiritual kinsman in the south, a century and more after him. Jeremiah's prophecy of the new covenant is itself a transference of emphasis from the external act to the inner spirit, as the only sphere in which a right relation between man and God can be established. Third in the great line comes the prophet of Nazareth, with the Sermon on the Mount, declaring that it is the lust within that is the essential sin, which He identifies with the outward act that expresses it.

To us it seems obvious that such a conception of sin individualizes it, and this, in fact, was seen by Jeremiah. It cannot be claimed that Hosea sees the full consequence of his own inner emphasis on the individual life. It is of the nation Israel, as a whole, that he is thinking, according to the sense of corporate personality which characterizes the thought of Israel. True, the deeds which he condemns are committed by individual persons, as his own experience of Gomer's conduct has amply shown. But it is the social mass of evil, the common stock to which each man contributes, that is primarily in his mind, and it is the common spirit, the spirit that prompts the whole people to such evil, which he discerns. We cannot speak of more than an implicit individualism in his phrase.

What shall we say, then, of the sense of individual responsibility for the evil? Here, also, the consequences of his insight are not drawn out by the prophet, in the manner of Ezekiel. In fact, there are distinct degrees of blame in the condemnations of Hosea. We have seen that his bitterest invective is directed against the priests, for their own misconduct and for their neglect of duty towards the people: "My people are destroyed for lack of knowledge; because thou hast rejected knowledge, I will also reject thee, that thou shalt be no priest to me" (4: 6). In such a differentiation of responsibility, we are near to the teaching of the Gospel, "that servant which knew his lord's will, and made not ready, nor did according to his will, shall be beaten with many stripes; but he that knew not, and did things worthy of stripes, shall be beaten with few stripes" (Luke 12: 47, 48). In every sin we commit, there is surely something of our own and something of the society in which we have grown up, and no human calculus is adequate to adjust the proportion of responsibility, though every man may come near to the knowledge of his own. The complexity of the assessment is all the more if we regard this earth as part of a larger order, as the Bible does, an order in which the good and evil of an invisible world play their part in influencing our conduct.

4. *The Atrophy of the Will*

That inner alienation of which we have been speaking is not only the source of evil deeds, it is also in increasing degree their consequence. This is one of the most subtle and most terrible aspects of sin, with which we are all familiar, an aspect that constantly recurs in literature. Writers who cannot be accused of theological prepossessions tell us as emphatically as they can that there is an atrophy of the will born of evil deeds. Here, for example, is Burns, speaking of sexual sin:

> *I wave the quantum o' the sin;*
> *The hazard of concealing;*
> *But Och! it hardens a' within,*
> *And petrifies the feeling!*

There is a deeply impressive story by Nathaniel Hawthorne, called *Ethan Brand*. It is the study of a man obsessed with the idea of the "Unpardonable Sin", who sets out on the quest of it, and finds it nowhere. He returns to his home, and finds it in his own heart—"The sin of an intellect that triumphed over the sense of brotherhood with man and reverence for God, and sacrificed everything to its own mighty claims." In the cold and unsympathetic quest, his own heart "had withered . . . had contracted . . . had hardened . . . had perished"! There is also a grim poem by Whittier, called *The Answer*, all the more memorable when we remember the gentle spirit of the man who wrote it:

> *No word of doom may shut thee out,*
> *No wind of wrath may downward whirl,*
> *No swords of fire keep watch about*
> *The open gates of pearl;*
>
> *A tenderer light than moon or sun,*
> *Than song of earth a sweeter hymn,*
> *May shine and sound forever on,*
> *And thou be deaf and dim.*
>
> *Forever round the Mercy-seat*
> *The guiding lights of Love shall burn;*
> *But what if, habit-bound, thy feet*
> *Shall lack the will to turn?*
>
> *What if thine eye refuse to see,*
> *Thine ear of Heaven's free welcome fail,*
> *And thou a willing captive be,*
> *Thyself thy own dark jail?*

Does Hosea, then, say this? Not in so many words, but it is implicit in some of his sayings: "Whoredom and wine and new wine take away the will" (literally, the heart, the seat of volition) (4: 11). . . . "Ephraim is

wedded to idols, let him alone" (4: 17). . . . "Their
doings will not suffer them to turn unto their God"
(5: 4). . . . "They became abominable like that which
they loved" (9: 10). Further, we may take his use of the
figure of sowing and reaping as indicating the closeness
of connection between the sin and its penalty, or some
of its penalty. Thus, in 10: 12, 13 he says:

> Sow to yourselves according to righteousness,
> Reap according to (your) piety. . . .
> Ye have ploughed wickedness,
> Ye have reaped injustice
> Ye have eaten the fruit of (your) lies.

This is an anticipation of Saint Paul's: "Whatsoever a
man soweth, that shall he also reap"; and of Emerson's
principle, in the great essay on *Compensation*: "Crime
and punishment grow out of one stem. Punishment is a
fruit that unsuspected ripens within the flower of the
pleasure which concealed it." The figure doubtless
implies much besides the moral atrophy of the sinner,
since the Hebrew principle of retribution and its con-
finement within the limits of this life demanded an
ultimate adjustment of outer circumstance to the inner
quality of the man. But it includes that moral deterioration, a deterioration which is asserted by other prophets
also. Isaiah at his call hears the words of commission in
the enigmatic terms: "Make the heart of this people fat,
and make their ears heavy, and shut their eyes; lest they
see with their eyes, and hear with their ears, and their
heart should understand and turn and be healed" (6:
10). Here, as we saw in the initial command to Hosea, the
consequences are automatically included in the commission, but the underlying assumption is that the
sequel of disobedience is the growing inability to obey.
So also in well-known words, Jeremiah asks:

*Can the Ethiopian change his skin, or the leopard his spots?
Then may ye also do good, that are trained to do evil.*

(13: 23.)

The Hebrew vocabulary for "sin" tells us the same thing. There are words that refer to some outer standard: such as those that speak of deviation from the right way; or the forfeiture of status that accompanies the judicial verdict of "guilty"; or an act of rebellion towards a superior; or of infidelity to an agreement; but there are a number of words also that characterize sin as "vice", i.e. as something that is bad in itself, before any external standard of judgment is applied. In this connection we may notice the striking figure of old age which is applied to Israel, the premature senility of the man who has abused his body: "Strangers have devoured his strength and he knoweth it not; yea, gray hairs are sprinkled upon him and he knoweth it not" (7: 9).

5. Sin Against the Background of Grace

Yet the truest and deepest revelation of the nature of sin does not come from its inner or outer consequences, but from its aspects when thrown up against the background of grace—the grace of God which has marked Israel's long history, and turns her present disposition and conduct into churlish ingratitude. Alike in the prophetic teaching of the Old Testament and in the apostolic teaching of the New, the sin of sins is ingratitude. That ingratitude is seen to its full extent only when God is conceived as the Father who has taught His little child to walk, and carried him when weary in His arms (11: 1 ff.): "though I have taught and strengthened their arms, yet do they imagine mischief against Me" (7: 15). . . . "Though I would redeem them, yet have they spoken lies against Me" (7: 13). That again is a recurrent note in the greater prophets, and prepares for the New Testament. How striking an expression of this is found in Paul's experience, when praying in the temple at the outset of his missionary work (Acts 22: 17). He sees two faces before him, the face of Stephen and the face of Christ. In that dramatic contrast of unforgotten sin and unforgettable grace, each is illuminated. If it is grace alone that can deal with the obdurate heart, so it is grace alone that reveals the sin of its obduracy. Gomer's infidelity takes on a new and darker colour against the fidelity of Hosea's love; his cross, like that of a greater Prophet, is the measure of human sin before it becomes the means of a divine salvation.

THE VICTORY OF GRACE

Hosea was not only the first discoverer of the inwardness of sin; he was also the pioneer of what may be called "Evangelical Realism". By this is meant that he fearlessly projected his own consciousness of a "gracious" attitude towards Gomer and his own experience of the cost of that grace into the consciousness of God. This projection, as we have seen, depends for its validity on the truth of the kinship of man and God; but if that is not in some sense true, we can say nothing at all about God. If it is true, then we dispose at once of the need for any transaction or legal fiction to reconcile God to man, since His love for man becomes our starting-point. But we also get a much deeper conception of the cost of grace to God, and we get rid of any superficial idea of grace as simply divine benevolence. If it costs so much to a man like Hosea to be gracious to a sinner, what must it not cost to God? More than this, we see more clearly from the example of Hosea why the New Testament so constantly insists that the believer in God's grace must necessarily be a lover of his brethren. You cannot really believe in the grace of God unless you are confident in its ultimate victory; but you cannot have that confidence from the outside of things. Unless you believe in the victory of grace over sin in your human relations, you cannot have any confidence about it in the divine. Hosea acted as he did towards Gomer because he was sure that the way of grace was the way of ultimate victory. That assurance is paralleled in his faith that God would be victorious through grace over the sin and sinfulness of Israel.

This conviction was deepened by his corresponding insight into the inwardness of sin. Because the root of sin was the spirit of infidelity far deeper than any particular act which expressed it, the remedy for sin must be something not less deep and vital—the cleansing and liberating power of a new spirit which should replace the old, and could be created only by its like. Amos had taught that the inevitable reaction of a holy God to sin must be judgment and the infliction of penalty; Hosea, not excluding penalty, but transforming it into discipline, makes that reaction to consist primarily in the suffering of grace, through the love that will not let the sinner go. Only this deeper way of grace could be the way of victory, for it alone was really spiritual in principal, and able to deal with the things of the spirit of man. This is evangelical realism. Instead of superimposing a theological structure, true or false, upon the events of history, it goes deeper into those events to find their intrinsic nature and their cosmic significance, whether they relate to the human or the divine. As Blake puts it:

> *God appears, and God is Light,*
> *To those poor souls who dwell in Night;*
> *But does a Human Form display*
> *To those who dwell in realms of Day.*

In this way alone can we hope to bring out the true continuity of the Old Testament and the New which has welded them both into the Christian Bible. They are one, because they both find God *in* man, and both bring the God they find *to* man. They are one, because, whatever the difference of scale and scope, the grace of our Lord Jesus Christ is of the same texture as the grace of the prophet Hosea.

1. *The Initiative of Grace*

The first great characteristic of that attitude and act which we call "grace" is its spontaneity; it takes the initiative, without waiting for anything that could warrant it. Thus the Epistle to the Ephesians (2: 4 ff.) declares that the exceeding riches of God's grace are shewn through His initial action in Christ, with whom we are raised to new life; "by grace have you been saved through faith, and that (salvation) is not from yourselves—of God is the gift; not from works, that no one may boast". A notable passage by Karl Holl claims this quality of initiative as the chief characteristic of the Christian faith, the quality that distinguishes it from all other religions: "We may say that Jesus reverses the usual relation of religion and morality. Every other religion, at any rate every religion of higher aims, bases the personal relation of God on the right conduct of man. The more moral anyone is—understanding 'moral' in the broadest sense, as including the cult—the nearer he stands to God. According to Jesus, it is, on the contrary, God who makes a beginning; it is He who posits a new thing in forgiveness. From it, however, there arises a real, close and warm relation to God, and at the same time a morality that can dare to take God Himself as its exemplar." (*Urchristentum und Religionsgeschichte*, p. 22.)

This quality of spontaneity is not denied by recognizing the real bond that unites God to man. Such bond can be of a lower or a higher kind. At the lowest level, it can indeed be conceived as the bargaining which we have just set in contrast with grace. At the higher, however, it springs from the compulsion of love, i.e. from the very nature of God Himself. This, surely, is *His* perfect freedom, to be able to be nothing but what He is. Thus, His covenant with Israel, on which the whole conception of Israel's religion rests, is not, for the prophets, a bargain at all. Amos repudiates the popular idea that Yahweh is mechanically bound to Israel as its God, and lifts the relation to the moral level. Hosea does far more; he lifts it to the level of the highest human relationships, viz. marriage and parenthood. He penetrates to that spirit of love which alone can fulfil the bond of the letter. For such a man, the covenant (*berith*), (2: 18; 6: 7; 8: 1) is the shell of which "loving-kindness" (*hesed*), (2: 19; 4: 1; 6: 4, 6; 10: 12; 12: 6) is the kernel. That great word "*hesed*" is very difficult to render, for it expresses the moral bondage of love, the loving discharge of an admitted obligation, the voluntary acceptance of a responsibility. It is significant that Amos does not use the term at all, whilst it occurs six times in Hosea. Its finest expression is in 11: 8, 9:

> *How shall I give thee up, Ephraim?*
> *How shall I deliver thee up, Israel?*
> *How shall I make thee as Admah?*
> *How shall I set thee as Zeboim?*
> *Mine heart is turned within me,*
> *My compassions are kindled together.*
> *I will not execute the fierceness of mine anger,*
> *I will not return to destroy Ephraim.*

That is the fundamental fact in the relation of God to Israel; He cannot let her go because He is what He is. He took the initiative with her, long ago, from the land of Egypt (13: 4); now, in her need, He takes a new initiative, like the old (2: 14–23). His first delight in His adopted child was as that of one who finds grapes in the wilderness, or the first-ripe fig (9; 10); but as a result of the new initiative, He can say: "From Me is thy fruit found" (14: 8). The terms of the new invitation are clearly expressed both at the beginning and the end of Hosea's prophecies: "I will betroth thee unto Me for ever; yea I will betroth thee unto Me in righteousness, and in justice and in loving-kindness and in mercies. I will even betroth thee unto Me in faithfulness: and thou shalt know Yahweh" (2: 19, 20). . . . "I will heal their backsliding, I will love them freely: for Mine anger is turned away from him" (14: 4).

This, then, is the Gospel according to Hosea. It is expressed, like that of the Prophet of Nazareth, in deeds as well as words; in fact, for both, it is true to say that the deed is the essential word, which the spoken syllables can only report. The symbolic act of the prophet, most of all when it moves on so high a level and involves such human relations as that of Hosea, becomes the very word of God. "I have spoken unto the prophets, and I have multiplied visions, and by the ministry of the prophets have I used similitudes" (12: 10). The first preaching of the Cross, for Hosea as well as for Jesus, is the Cross itself. In both, the personal initiative, under moral compulsion alone, is made evident; in both, the visible deed is made the witness and token to the invisible reality: "Go yet, love a woman beloved of her friend and an adulteress, even as Yahweh loveth the children of Israel, though they turn unto other gods." . . . "God commendeth His own love toward us, in that, while we were yet sinners, Christ died for us" (Hos. 3: 1; Rom. 5: 8).

2. The Redemptive Work of Grace

Can we carry further the analogy, or as I prefer to say, the intrinsic relation between the Cross of Hosea and the Cross of Christ? Can we go on to speak of the redemptive work of Hosea in relation to Gomer, with the full consciousness that we find in it something akin to the redemptive work of Christ? Let us look more closely at what is recorded in the third chapter of Hosea. He tells us that he had to purchase her, perhaps from the slavery of sanctuary-prostitution, at a slave's ransom.

The price was fifteen pieces of silver, and a homer and a half of barley, which is thought to be the equivalent of the thirty shekels at which a male or female slave was rated in Hebrew law (Exod. 21: 32). Given the circumstances, this was obviously a necessary step in the process of her recovery. Yet it is an accidental element in the redemptive work, which was essentially spiritual. The Salvation Army, on occasion, have purchased Chinese girls at 30s. a head, from their parents, in order to save them from a life of shame. But the really redemptive work was in the purpose to train these girls under Christian influences to a life of virtue. The act of grace was in the intention which informed the visible deed. So we should rightly say of Hosea that his purpose to save Gomer, by whatever means, was the essential expression of grace. The price paid for the execution of that purpose was spiritual rather than material, though the two are never wholly separated in our mingled life of body and soul. The spiritual price can be measured only in terms of suffering. When a holy will takes to itself, and accepts the burden of responsibility for an unholy will, there is the inevitable condition that the sin is transformed in the consciousness of the holy man into suffering; he cannot share its burden on any other terms. There is the suffering of actual contact with it, which Henry Drummond experienced as the repulsion of a cleanly person from physical filth; there is the suffering of inward association as well as the shame and disgrace which outward association may bring. There is the suffering which the very etymology of the word "patience" suggests, the struggle against disappointment and disillusionment and the temptation to abandon a hopeless quest. There is the sacrifice of so much that might have been, but for this perhaps thankless task. All these and more will be known to anyone who has honestly tried to redeem a life with which he owns solidarity and for which he accepts responsibility. The holier he is, the more will be his suffering. This is the constant law of holy grace, whether in man or God. Because it is grace, it cannot stand aloof and disclaim association with the sinner; because it is holy, it can associate itself with him only on terms of suffering.

All that is true of Jesus, in His own far greater way. However we are to conceive His redemptive work, that work was wrought out essentially through spiritual sufferings, whilst their physical accompaniments are little more than the occasion or expression of the spiritual. Would not the daily association with the alienated spirit of Judas be a crown of thorns to Him far more painful than that He wore in the judgment-hall? Was not Gethsemane His real Calvary? The best of us can get but a glimpse now and then of what it means to be holy with and among sinners, who yet may not be disowned and avoided. But we cannot say these things of Jesus and call them part of His redemptive work without recognizing the similarity of His experience with the saints of God before and after Him at whatever lower level. Whatever is intrinsically true of the redemptive suffering of Jesus must be true in its own degree of all the suffering of holy grace, such as is before us in Hosea's experience.

In what sense, then, can all such holy suffering be called redemptive in the full sense? That is, not simply as constituting a pathetic appeal to the sinner, powerful and essential as that appeal must be, but as "atoning" for the sin. There are two distinct aspects of it. There is the actual transformation of the evil of suffering (for suffering is an evil) in the saint; the transformation which makes the voluntary acceptance of that suffering an act of grace, full of gracious beauty. This transformation is quite distinct from the possible transformation of the sinner himself, of which we shall have to speak later. Whether or not that takes place, this is secure; an ugly thing has been made beautiful. All sin is ugly, and all grace is graceful, when the sin is sin and the grace is grace. (Here we note in passing a hint of ultimate reconciliation between the aesthetic and the ethical standards and interests.) As we look at the ugliness of Gomer's sin passing into the consciousness of Hosea to be transformed into a beauty that anticipates that of the Gospel, shall we not say that one element of atonement is present? We can never justify sin by its results; but this is the reversal of those results, the creation of a new spiritual gain that far transcends the loss incurred by the sin.

The other aspect, the other element in the atoning work of holy suffering, is raised when we ask what is the worth of this value to God. How does it concern Him that the suffering of the saint can thus transform evil into good? If we speak anthropomorphically, we can say that it is a sacrifice with which He is well pleased, an offering that is the truest worship, since it is the fullest recognition of His holy worth. But directly we try to work out our anthropomorphic metaphors, such as sacrifice, ransom, vicarious penalty, into some sort of theory, we get into difficulties. They are true, or they express a truth, in showing that the sinner cannot atone for his own sin. They are false whenever they suggest such a real gulf between man and God as has to be bridged by means external to Himself, or such an attitude of alienation as demands propitiation before He is gracious. But there is a deeper view, however impossible it be to rationalize or systematize it. If a prophet can identify himself with God, so that he suffers with the suffering of God over the sin of Israel, how much more will it be true that God suffers in the suffering of His prophets? The actuality of their suffering is part of His suffering; their crosses are gathered up into one great cross for Him; the spiritual values they achieve are His, through that intimate and inexpressible union of God and His saints, imperfect in them, but perfected in His Son. He is what Isaiah calls Him, the great burden-bearer (46: 1–4), because in Him we live and move and have our being; because He is immanent as well as transcendent. In the mystery of man's life within God, sinner or saint, God bears the sin through suffering, and shares the burden with His saints. If we have rightly understood the story of Hosea's life, he not only appeals to Gomer by the declaration of his unbroken love, but tries to help her practically towards recovery of her lost place. But he does more than this; he suffers with her and for her. Indeed, it may be said quite properly that he suffers far more than she can, just because of his forgiving love. Shall we not say, with Professor H. R. Mackintosh, that the forgiveness of God "must prove as full, as unqualified and overpowering in generosity, as the forgiveness of good men"? In man, as in God, true forgiveness *costs* something. Its measure may be partly seen in the attempt of the good man to raise the fallen, as a real element in his forgiveness. But behind the visible acts of helpfulness and reconciliation, there is an inner cost, a suffering born from sacrificial love, a suffering greater in the saint than in the sinner, and surely greatest in God. Thus we may speak, with Bushnell, of "a cross in God before the wood is seen upon Calvary" (*The Vicarious Sacrifice*, p. 35). To identify the atonement ultimately with the sacrificial love of God is not to minimize in the least the significance of the Cross of Christ in history, for that becomes the supreme actualization in time of the truth that holds for all eternity. But this way of facing the doctrine of atone-ment does remove it from the category of a transaction, a mere event, a sort of device belonging to the "plan of salvation". Atonement now becomes something deep-based in the very nature of God, as natural to Him as the forgiving love of a human saint. If it be true that in God we live and move and have our being, then our sins must somehow be conceived within the circle of His holiness. Yet how can they be conceived there save as suffering within the Godhead—suffering for man, penal, disciplinary, chastening; and suffering for God, sacrificial, redemptive; and, at last, transformed into the joy of triumph? We should like to know whether the suffering love of Hosea did avail to win back the sinning Gomer, but, whether it did or not, that suffering love has transformed a sordid story into a prophecy of the Gospel. Similarly, the sacrificial love of God is always faced by the mystery of human personality and freedom, and none can declare the issue of its appeal to the individual; but the love behind it transforms the meaning of the world's history and makes it glorious with the "iridescent" wisdom of God (Eph. 3: 10).

3. *The Discipline of Grace*

When the inwardness of Israel's sin was under consideration, our thought was confined to the inward penalty, that atrophy of the spirit of man which sin inevitably induces. This essential separation from God is always the real penalty of sin. But the external and visible penalty occupies a large part of the prophecies of Hosea. Under many figures he describes the wrath of God against sin, and the penalty which falls on it. Yahweh is compared with the lion, the leopard and the bear that attack the defenceless prey (13: 7, 8), or the fowler who snares the bird in his net (7: 12) or the destroying moth (5: 12). The doom of Israel is represented as inexorable: "Shall I ransom them from the power of Sheol? Shall I redeem them from death? O death where are thy plagues? O Sheol where is thy destruction?" (13: 14). The exact nature of this destruction is again made clear in numerous passages. It is war and invasion and all the sufferings they bring, whether from Assyria or from Egypt, the two great powers on the horizon, and it will end in exile: "Ephraim shall return to Egypt, and they shall eat unclean food in Assyria" (9: 3); "they shall be wanderers among the nations" (9: 17); "the Assyrian shall be his king" (11: 5); "Egypt shall gather them up" (9: 6). It is immaterial to the prophet whether the destruction come from Assyria or Egypt; he is not concerned with foretelling events, like an "Old Moore's" Almanack, but with declaring the certain and inevitable penalty of sin, in the shame and desolation, the disorder and helplessness, the utter overthrow of all the strong places in which the nation trusted (10: 14; 11: 6). He may have witnessed the harrowing scenes of the deportation of 732 B.C.

Yet we should miss the real meaning of these prophecies of judgment, if we forgot what we have already emphasized—the divine purpose to save. The penalty is certain, but only if the sin endures. Yahweh has withdrawn Himself, but only "till they have borne their guilt and seek My face" (5: 15). The individual members of the nation are bidden to plead with their mother, the nation in its corporate personality: "lest I strip her naked" (2: 3). The final chapter visualizes a genuine repentance and return, in which the nation seeks healing from Him who has smitten (6: 1; cf. 14: 4). It is clear, therefore, that the penalty is meant to be pedagogic; it is intended to secure repentance, and cannot be rightly estimated as mere retribution, though its retributive aspect is so strongly emphasized. Even as penalty, it falls within the covenant of grace, and gets its meaning from the ultimate purpose of God.

We must beware, then, here, as whenever such themes are discussed, lest we deny or minimize the reality of the wrath of God against sin, or conceive of that wrath as propitiated by the smoking altars and the costly gifts. That is what the ordinary Israelite thought, but it is the very thing which the greater prophets condemned. They were struggling to express their conviction that divine retribution is a reality, carried out according to moral principles. That is true for Amos; but Hosea, without any abandonment of it, proclaims a higher morality of "loving-kindness". The result of this is that penalty may be transformed into discipline. That is what it certainly is in the purpose of God; that is what it must surely become in all who turn to Him, i.e. who come to share in His purpose. We need not ask whether the retributive element is exact—the problem that troubled Israelite thinkers so greatly in the later days, when the corporate personality of the nation was modified by a new individualism, which asked how the individual experience could be shown to be one of exact retribution. In Hosea's time, the nation is the unit, and the later problem has not emerged. If one generation does not see the work of Yahweh, then another will; that suffices.

The really important aspect of penalty is its potential effect on the sinner who encounters it—a truth which need not and ought not to hide from us that some penalties are inexorable, even in the course of an outward order of events. Thus, a nation that has gone so far down the slippery slope of civil strife, conspiracy and disorder as Israel could hardly have escaped from Assyria, however ardent her repentance; a woman who had fallen like Gomer could never recover her innocence. The point that must not be missed is that a true repentance which enters into God's purpose will accept the penalty that continues after such repentance, but will transform it into willingly accepted discipline. This is the implicit hope behind Hosea's treatment of Gomer in Chapter 2, when she is separated for the "many days" of discipline, before the old relations with her husband can be resumed. This is what the great prophet of the Exile learnt so well, when he bade his fellow-country-men consecrate their sufferings into a sacrificial offering, through which the nations of the world might be not only moved to penitence but also enabled to approach God through the sacrifice. The unit of experience is always the outer event plus the inner attitude; for the outer event has meaning only in the light of that inner attitude, and that inner attitude has power to transform the worst into the best.

4. *The Response to Grace*

Finally, we have to consider the victory of grace in the heart of the penitent sinner, the culminating point of the whole appeal and work of grace. Here, it can be said that: "The great teacher at once of the necessity and the value of true repentance was Hosea, who dwelt upon it positively, as though no more was needed" (Welch, *Post-Exilic Judaism*, p. 301). The reference of the "no more" in this sentence is to the cult, and its context makes a contrast with Isaiah and Micah, who "developed the theme with a conscious reference to the demands of the cult". Hosea's attitude is most concisely expressed in the words quoted on two occasions by Jesus, viz.: "I delight in mercy and not in sacrifice; and the knowledge of God more than burnt offerings" (6: 6; cf. Matt. 9: 13; 12: 7). Here the word rendered "mercy" (*hesed*) can mean either piety towards God or kindness towards man, and perhaps includes both here. The sentence does not necessarily form a condemnation of the cult, any more than its quotation by Jesus implied this (cf. Mark 1: 44); but it does imply a very different emphasis, and the primary need of repentance manifested in changed conduct. This true and deep repentance

56

is contrasted with the superficial and inadequate repentance described in the previous verses of the chapter: "Come and let us return unto Yahweh." Those who say this are less concerned with their sin than with their afflictions, and are quite sure that the mere appeal to God who has smitten them will produce an instant change of attitude in Him; and that His favour and help are as certain as to-morrow's dawn, or as the autumnal and spring rains. With great artistic effect, the prophet reveals Yahweh taking up these comparisons by two others which represent the fickleness of the "piety" offering this so-called repentance: "Your piety is as the morning cloud, and as the night-mist that goeth early away." We might compare its superficiality with that of the dying Heine's jest: "Dieu me pardonnera; c'est son métier." With this is purposely contrasted that fine expression of a true and lasting penitence which the prophet puts by anticipation in the mouth of Israel. This liturgy of the confession of sin and of the declaration of grace has been rightly made the culminating point of the book (14). It begins with the prophet's invitation, and his appeal to the discipline of experience (1). Then he frames for Israel the words in which the evil of the old paths may be confessed, making articulate their inarticulate needs, which now replace the former glib approach to God. The "fruit of their lips" is still what they offer (2 RVm.), but it is now a true offering, for it is marked by definite and actual renunciation of the false helps and material aids of the past: "Asshur shall not save us; we will not ride upon horses: neither will we say any more to the work of our hands, Ye are our gods" (3). So comes the answer of grace: "I will heal. . . . I will love them freely" (4). The restored prosperity of Israel is described in figures of natural beauty (5-7), and there is a closing antiphony in which Ephraim cries: "What have I to do any more with idols?" and Yahweh replies:

"I have answered, and will regard him"; Ephraim declares "I am like a green fir tree"; and Yahweh gives what is at once a warning and a promise "From Me is thy fruit found". It would be difficult to find in the whole Bible a truer programme of penitence and grace expressed in their interaction.

But all this raises the important question: what is to secure this deep and actual penitence, whether in Gomer or in the nation of which she is a representative product? The two parts of the question are one. Nor are we to unite them simply as though Gomer were an external object-lesson of grace, to which the prophet could point and say: "God's attitude towards Israel is like this of mine towards Gomer." True as that would be to his conception, it would not at all adequately express its inner logic. We have to think here, as so often, of that category of corporate personality which is always conditioning the status of the individual in Biblical times. Gomer is more than what *we* mean by a symbol: she is for the time being the epitome of Israel. In her centres and culminates (for the prophet) the physical sexuality and the spiritual infidelity of Israel; in her, if his appeal of love be not in vain, will be found the first-fruits of the new harvest, the promise and potency of a genuine repentance. The conversion of Gomer will be an actual event, part of, and instrumental to, the conversion of Israel. The symbolical acts of the prophets have, all of them, in greater or less degree, this quality of not merely *representing* the whole act of God, but of being a veritable part of it. If we say that this belongs to a stage of thought at which there was a defective sense of individual personality, that is true enough; yet such a stage may serve to show a real truth about the solidarity of the race, which the sheer individualism of modern times may easily miss. This is the counterpoise to the obvious weakness of appealing to a whole nation for what must be a series of individual repentances. Hosea's appeal is both individual and national, because *his first objective in Gomer is both*. Thus, the remembrance of this important category of ancient thought removes the apparent artificiality of making a domestic sorrow into a prophetic symbol; restores the actuality of life to the whole conduct and message of the prophet, and points forward to that death unto sin and resurrection unto life, which Paul saw as wrought out for us all in Christ.

Even so, how pathetic does the frailty of the appeal seem, when matched against the vested interests and the settled habits of a people, in which each sinning individual is entrenched, as Gomer was! From the standpoint of reason, the preaching of such a prophet was as much foolishness as the Cross—because it was of the same nature. It is a spiritual appeal that matches itself in Quixotic romance against all these things; but its strength is that it *is* spiritual, and alone able to grapple with the spiritual fact of the inwardness of sin. A Jew has put into the mouth of a Jew the words: "Christianity is Judaism run divinely mad" (Zwangwill, *Dreamers of the Ghetto*, p. 324). Certainly, there is real continuity with the Gospel in the evangelical appeal of Hosea. It is an impossible one, except for those who believe in the power of love; for those who so believe with all their heart and soul, it is the only possible appeal. A magistrate told me of a striking example of this. One Saturday, he had before him a girl charged with solicitation. He pleaded with her to abandon her dreadful trade, but in vain, though he offered to arrange for a new start in life for her. Finally, he adjourned the case till Monday. On the Sunday, something moved him to write a letter to her, and with it he sent a bunch of flowers. Some time after both had been delivered, the wardress entered the cell, and found the girl lying on the floor and sobbing bitterly. All she would say was: "He sent me flowers, he sent me flowers." On Monday she was docile and ready to try again, and, as the years proved, not in vain.

One more question may be asked. What is the relation of the inner to the outer restoration? How far is true repentance accompanied by the full return of prosperity? The promises of Hosea are quite definite; he anticipates that the new betrothal (2: 19 ff.) will be followed by such harmony of outer nature as will supply all Israel's physical needs. In what we should call a series of cause and effect, the appeal of Israel is passed on by the corn and wine and oil to the earth from which they spring, and from the earth to the heavens that give the fertilizing and necessary rains; and from the heavens to Him who controls their store-houses, and who promises to respond to the appeal. Here, as in the Epilogue to Job, the destiny of men must be wrought out, and the divine righteousness vindicated, in the visible life of earth, since there is no horizon of real life beyond death. The extension of that horizon to include the unseen, as in the Christian hope of immortality, provides an ampler arena for that vindication. At long last, the righteousness, which, for Hosea, includes the loving-kindness of God, must be fully vindicated; and forgiveness must be made visible, and reconciliation demonstrated. We may remember that such a hope enters into Paul's vision, when he speaks of the whole creation groaning and travailing in pain together until now, waiting for its deliverance from the bondage of corruption (Rom. 8: 21, 22). So, in society, it is as impossible to divorce the vision of a Kingdom of God on earth from the life and activities of the saints, as it is to limit their lives and activities by such a kingdom. All we dare to say is that grace must be victorious in every realm, the earthly and the heavenly. Whatever happens in the future pilgrimage of man's spirit, the essential things must depend on the inner attitude, creative of the meaning of all that befalls it. The Gospel of Hosea is that of a love able to transform life by creating a new attitude within, leading to a new interpretation of all things without, a new meaning. For spiritual beings, all that ultimately matters is the meaning of things, and man's spirit is capable of any miracle of transformation, when once aroused to its task. The great idea of love must be wrought out in life to become actual and so effective. It was made actual first through the Cross of Hosea; it culminated in the Cross of Christ, and it is continued in the countless other crosses of God's prophets and apostles in all generations.

The Visions of Ezekiel

Commentaries referred to:

Battersby Harford, J., *Studies in the Book of Ezekiel*, 1935.

Bertholet, A., *Hesekiel*, 1936 (chapters 40-48 by K. Galling).

Cooke, G. A., *The Book of Ezekiel, International Critical Commentary*, 1936.

Herntrich, V., *Ezechielprobleme*, 1932.

Herrmann, J., *Ezechiel*, 1924.

Hölscher, G., *Hesekiel*, 1924.

Smith, James, *The Book of Ezekiel, a New Interpretation*, 1931.

Torrey, C. C., *Pseudo-Ezekiel*, 1930.

THE HISTORICAL BACKGROUND AND
LITERARY CRITICISM

In the ancient world, politics and religion were much more closely linked than for ourselves; indeed, they were often but different aspects and interpretations of the same events. The fortunes of a State depended on the conduct of its citizens and rulers, but those fortunes were also bound up with the will of the gods. Religion was primarily concerned with the maintenance of right relations with the gods; it was not a personal and private affair which a man might carry on independently of his neighbour, nor was it closely bound up with such moral ideas as the nation possessed. When we speak, therefore, of the historical background of an ancient book we are not describing tapestry hangings on the walls, which simply give colour to the scene; we must think rather of the courtyard of a castle with living figures advancing and withdrawing, all of them concerned with both political and religious interests, even though some were primarily what we should call politicians, and others prophets or priests.

1. *Politics and Religion*

This close interplay of politics and religion can be seen in particular all through that century of Judah's history which leads up to the life of Ezekiel, as well as in that life itself. The withdrawal of Sennacherib in 701 B.C. left a desolated Judah, and Hezekiah may have got the credit of a destruction of the high places which was really due to the Assyrian invader (2 Kings 18: 4); it would not be the only occasion on which religion had claimed for its own what was due to the economic and military forces of the world. Through most of the seventh century, Judah remained a vassal State to Assyria. This political relation largely explains the syncretistic religion of the Judaeans in the time of Manasseh from 691 to 638. It is described by the prophet Zephaniah at the end of the reign as including the worship of the host of heaven upon the housetops (1: 4-6), which means, of course, the recognition of the Assyrian State religion alongside of the native Yahwism (cf. 2 Kings 21: 3-6). This would be taken for granted in those days by the ordinary man; political subjection meant religious syncretism, just as any struggle for political freedom would include religious motives also. What such syncretism might involve we have learnt from the Elephantine papyri; the smiling colony there may go back indeed to Israel's relations with Egypt in the seventh century, and reflect the religious conditions of Israel itself.

We get another illustration of the inter-relation of politics and religion in the Josianic Reformation, which followed upon the long reign of Manasseh and the short reign of his son Amon. There is no question of Josiah's religious sincerity but he naturally expected that a reformer's zeal would be followed by a politician's success. In fact, the reformation itself was rendered possible only by the decline of Assyrian power, of which the first sign had been the Scythian invasion of a few years previous. Josiah's activities extended to Bethel, that is, into the Assyrian province which the northern kingdom had become; this would have been impossible whilst Assyria was strong. Similarly, when Josiah advanced northwards to oppose an Egyptian army under Pharaoh Necho at Megiddo in 608, he could have had no Assyrian opposition in the Assyrian province that had replaced the former northern kingdom to threaten his line of communications. He was probably fighting in faith that Yahweh would secure to His people the new-won liberty, whilst, as we have learnt from the Gadd tablet, the Egyptians were coming to the help of Assyria, which had continued to struggle on even after the fall of Nineveh in 612. The defeat and death of Josiah at Megiddo in 608 meant a violent popular reaction from the faith of his reformation. It had not brought political success; what, then, was the good of it? Men should go back and worship in the sensible way of their forefathers and hope for better things! We know from both Jeremiah and Ezekiel that worship on the high places and many alien elements in worship returned, derived from Mesopotamia and Egypt (Jer. 7: 18, 13: 27; Ezek. 8: 10).

Events in Judah during the generation preceding the fall of Jerusalem in 586, which is the pivot of Ezekiel's prophetic activities, as it is the culmination of those of Jeremiah, can be understood only if we keep the imperial backgrounds in mind. Josiah was succeeded by his son, Jehoahaz (Shallum), who was displaced by Pharaoh after a three months' reign in favour of his elder brother, Eliakim (who may have been passed over as a pro-Egyptian in the first instance). Pharaoh changed his name to Jehoiakim, whom Jeremiah denounces for his exactions and luxurious life; did he not live in a large house with roof-chambers, panelled with cedar and painted with vermilion? (22: 13–19)—a very different man from his father, Josiah. But in 605, three years after Megiddo, Pharaoh was overthrown by Nebuchadrezzar at Carchemish. Jehoiakim seems to have been left alone for some years but inevitably became subject to Babylon, as soon as Nebuchadrezzar had time to attend to him. After three years of vassaldom to Babylon, Jehoiakim rebelled, but died before the Babylonian king could come to exact vengeance. This fell in 597 on his son, Jehoiachin, who, like his uncle, Jehoahaz, reigned for three months only. Jehoahaz had been deported to Egypt; under the changed conditions, Jehoiachin was taken as a prisoner to Babylon, where his captivity was not relaxed until 561. The fates of the two royal princes are described in one of Ezekiel's poems, which may be quoted as an example of the way in which a poetical prophet could describe political events. It is in the form of a dirge, the mother of the two princes being Judah (19: 1–9):

> *Ah! your mother was a lioness*
> *in the midst of lions;*
> *She couched among young lions,*
> *she reared her whelps.*
> *She brought up one of her whelps,*
> *a young lion he became;*
> *He learned to catch the prey,*
> *mankind he devoured.*
> *The nations raised a clamour against him,*
> *in their pit was he taken;*
> *They led him away with hooks*
> *to the land of Egypt.*
>
> *When she saw that she was foiled,*
> *that her hope was gone,*
> *She took another of her whelps,*
> *a young lion she made him.*
> *He stalked among lions,*
> *a young lion he became;*
> *He learned to catch the prey,*
> *mankind he devoured.*
> *He ravaged their palaces,*
> *and their cities he laid waste;*
> *The land was awed and all who were in it,*
> *at the sound of his roaring.*
>
> *Against him the nations placed*
> *their snares round about;*

> *They spread their net for him,*
> * in their pit was he taken.*
> *They placed him in a cage,*
> * they brought him under guard;*
> *And they led him away with hooks*
> * to the King of Babylon;*
> *That his voice might be heard no more*
> * on the mountains of Israel.*
>
> (Gordon in American Trans.)

Jehoiachin was succeeded by Zedekiah, whom Ezekiel condemns for his breach of the oath of loyalty to the King of Babylon (17: 12 ff.). This weak king, whose character we see clearly enough in the light of Jeremiah's dealings with him, made an ineffective revolt in 594, and a much more serious one, supported from Egypt, some years later. This led to Nebuchadrezzar's campaign against Jerusalem and the fall of the city in 586. Ezekiel has given us a vivid picture of an incident on the march (21: 18 ff.). He described Nebuchadrezzar standing where the roads divide to Jerusalem and to Ammon, a momentary ally of Judah. "The king of Babylon stands at the parting of the ways, at the fork of the two roads, practising divination; he shakes the arrows, he consults the teraphim, he inspects the liver. Into his right hand falls the lot marked 'Jerusalem', calling for slaughter, for the shout of battle, for the planting of battering-rams against the gates, for the throwing-up of mounds, for the building of a siege wall." The prophet himself gave a mimic representation of that siege, which became, as has been said, the pivot of his prophetic activities, the central fact in his interpretation of history.

From this historical background, we now turn to the difficult but inevitable subject of literary criticism, which is still in a very debatable stage.

2. The Problems of the Book and Some Attempted Solutions

The Book of Ezekiel is probably the most neglected of the prophetic writings, so far as Christian readers of the Old Testament are concerned. The reasons for that neglect are not far to seek. The Book is largely written in prose, and its prose is often very prosy, lacking the simple charm of much Hebrew narrative and the striking metaphors of Hebrew poetry. There are many monotonous repetitions, and the subject-matter often seems remote from our living interests. Then the prophet himself strikes us as an odd sort of person, doing strange things, even childish things; how can we fit such a man into our own world-outlook? Finally, the teaching of the book, when we do arrive at it, offers a conception of God as one who is more concerned to exalt His own honour by the destruction of the nations than to redeem them. Certainly, Ezekiel is not the book with which you would begin, if you wanted to interest a newcomer in the Old Testament.

These disadvantages found some compensation in the fact that the Book of Ezekiel until recently seemed to escape from the critical fortunes of its companions.[1] A generation or two ago, the commentaries and exposition of the Book of Ezekiel went straight ahead in the cheerful confidence that here, at least, there was no question of a Deutero- or Trito-Ezekiel. You started off at the first verse with the prophet definitely located in Babylon amongst the exiles; and, except for two wholly visionary

[1] The subsequent discussion was written before Dr. Robinson had seen *The Problem of Ezekiel*, by W. A. Irwin, 1943, but his criticism of that book as too subjective to offer any "material contribution to the elucidation of Ezekiel" (in *Journal of Theol. Studies*, July–October 1944) shows that the argument would have remained unaffected by it. Nor had he seen I. G. Matthews in *An American Commentary on the Old Testament*, Philadelphia, 1939.

expeditions to the homeland, there he remained to the end, first holding forth on the sure destruction of the distant Jerusalem, and, after its fall, speaking to the exiles of its future restoration, and even planning out in detail what that restoration would be. Not only so, but it seemed that, for the first time in prophecy, the prophet had kept a diary of his prophecies, with precise dates of utterance, as though to silence any future questioning, and to warn off the critics from trespassing on this domain at any rate.

Alas, there began to rise clouds on the critical horizon. Closer examination of the book showed that its apparently chronological order was not so exact as it seemed. The dates did not cover all the intervening material. There is, for example, in Chapter 3 (16–21), the appointment of the prophet as watchman, which comes between the two dates of July 593, in Chapter 1 (1; at the end of seven days, 3: 16), and September 592, in Chapter 8 (1); yet is clearly dated by its subject-matter as belonging after 586, when the city had fallen (33: 21). The repetitions began to look suspiciously like different versions of the same prophetic message. Thus, to take a short example, in Chapter 7, verses 2–4 and 5–9 are identical in meaning, and to some extent in expression; such occurrences, which are very frequent, suggest that someone has collected differing memories of the same utterance. In Chapter 30: 20–26, we even get three references in similar terms to the breaking of the arms of Pharaoh and the strengthening of those of the King of Babylon in such a way as could come from three parallel versions of the same oracle (so Bertholet, p. 109). Such phenomena point at least to considerable editorial work on the text of Ezekiel, and leave us to infer that things are not so straightforward as was assumed. In fact, Herrmann, whose commentary appeared in 1924, and who was largely followed by G. A. Cooke in his commentary of 1936, whilst retaining the substantial authorship of the Babylonian Ezekiel, recognized that considerable additions have been made to his work.

A much more drastic solution was sought by Hölscher. In his history of the religion of Israel published in 1922, followed up by a special book on Ezekiel in 1924, he sharply distinguished the true Ezekiel as a poet from the writers of the prose portions of the book who belong to the next century. This would leave to Ezekiel not more than one-eighth of the present book. Hölscher's method and results have not found any general acceptance; they are too arbitrary and subjective. There is no sound reason why we should require a prophet always to speak in rhythmic form, though this was peculiarly suited to the prophetic oracle.

There were, however, other ways of attacking the problem, and particularly a remarkable feature of it which has not yet been mentioned. If Ezekiel prophesied in Babylon, as we are told in the opening verses, how is it that the first half of his book is so largely concerned with events in Jerusalem and Judaea in the interval be-between 593 and 586? These do not read like utterances from a distance. Some of them, as in Chapters 8–11, are full of contemporary detail, implying the knowledge of someone on the spot. Ezekiel's memories of conditions before 597, when he was assumed to have been carried into exile, might supply some of this information, and he might possibly have heard news from travellers. But such suppositions hardly satisfy the particularity of these references. In fact, the general assumption has been to credit the prophet with unusual powers of telepathy and clairvoyance. We have also a number of remarkable symbolical actions performed by the prophet, which would seem to lose their point when so far removed from the very people they concerned, the Israelites remaining in Jerusalem and Judaea. Also we are left asking how the prophet's oracles to the "rebellious house" (his favourite name for the Judaeans) could actually reach them, if merely reported to the exiles. It would be unlike a prophet not to give his message to those whom it directly concerned.

Such considerations inspired a new approach. In 1931, James Smith put forward the theory that Ezekiel was really a prophet of the Northern Kingdom, carried into exile in 693, that is, in "the thirtieth year" after 722, the date of the fall of Samaria. He was allowed to return to Palestine, and continued prophesying there or amongst the northern exiles until 669. In support of this theory, Smith appealed to the conditions in the time of Manasseh as a much more suitable background for Ezekiel's prophecies than Judaea after the Deuteronomic reformation (note the many denunciations of idolatry). He also pointed to the frequent use of the phrase "house of Israel" as properly denoting the northern and not the southern kingdom. This view has the advantage of bringing the prophet into actual relation with those he addresses, but it has failed to convince. As Battersby Harford has shown, the phrase "house of Israel" does not bear the meaning given to it by Smith, and there is evidence to show that after the death of Josiah in 608 there was a popular revulsion of feeling, and a resort to the old paganism. People said to Jeremiah: "When we left off to burn incense to the queen of heaven, and to pour out drink offerings unto her, we have wanted all things, and have been consumed by the sword and by famine" (Jer. 44: 18). It might well be, therefore, that things were just as bad in Jerusalem in Ezekiel's time as they had been in the time of Manasseh.

A Protestant might think of the parallel offered by the Marian reaction to Roman Catholicism after the Edwardian reformation in this country.

In the year before Smith's book appeared, viz. in

1930, though without influencing him, Torrey brought out a more complicated theory, inspired by his general purpose to discredit the historicity of the Babylonian exile. He regards the Book of Ezekiel as a product of the Greek period, written not long before the time of Ben Sira. The writer of this "Pseudo-Ezekiel" threw back his imagination to the time of Manasseh, and wrote as a prophet might have written if living under that king and denouncing the contemporary idolatry (cf. the method of the apocalyptists). The "thirtieth year" is the thirtieth year of Manasseh's reign, which dates the fiction as 663 B.C. But, not many years after the actual writing of the book in its original form, say about 230 B.C., the composition was converted into a Babylonian prophecy amongst the exiles, as part of the Jewish propaganda against the Samaritans. The true Israel, according to the theory of this propagandist, was preserved only in Babylonia. It is not surprising that Torrey's theory appears to be confined practically to himself, and is likely to pass, like his similar theory about Deutero-Isaiah, into the melancholy museum of critical aberrations.

The solid ground in all these reconstructions is that much of the first half of the Book of Ezekiel is intrinsically more likely to have been given in Palestine than in Babylon. On this ground, Herntrich built in 1932, and he has been largely followed by Battersby Harford in 1935. Ezekiel was not a Babylonian prophet at all; his historical sphere was Jerusalem, though editorial work has subsequently transferred this into a Babylonian frame. The foreign prophecies and the temple-restoration belong to a period later than that of Ezekiel.

So far, then (apart from Hölscher's separation of the poetry from the prose), we have had three types of theory in modification of the prima facie and conventional view of the book. The first, that of Herrmann and Cooke, still maintained Babylonian authorship and substantial integrity, though with considerable editorial additions or rearrangements to meet some of the difficulties of this view. The second, that of Smith and Torrey placed the book either before or after the exile, but in Palestine. The third, that of Herntrich and Battersby Harford, kept Ezekiel in Judaea, whilst relegating much of the book to the exilic or post-exilic period. Clearly, a fourth possibility remains—that the historic Ezekiel prophesied in both Judaea and Babylon. This is the view taken by Bertholet in 1936, and I have been slowly driven to the conclusion that this is the most likely of all the theories, whilst it certainly provides the best working hypothesis, so long as critical uncertainty remains. Let us look, then, more closely at Bertholet's statement of the case. He is building, of course, on what I have called the solid ground of the close relation of the first half of the book with the people and events of Judaea and Jerusalem.

3. Ezekiel Prophet of Judah and Babylon

The corner-stone of Bertholet's structure is that the book opens with two distinct calls to prophecy, instead of one. The call to prophesy in Babylon, involving the vision of the throne-chariot, has been placed in the first chapter, though actually coming later than the call to prophesy in Jerusalem, which describes the eating of the written roll in the second and third chapters. This change of order was natural enough if the prophet's later work was in Babylon, because this became the more inclusive standpoint. We may compare the way in which the later account of creation (Gen. 1) now precedes the earlier, in Chapter 2. The second call was necessary, because the fall of Jerusalem in 586 was an overwhelming event, demanding a new adjustment, and because it was an innovation for a prophet's experience to come in a strange land, an innovation which demanded a special guarantee from Yahweh Himself. He needed and obtains a precise command to go to the exiles as a prophet (3: 11).

Bertholet's reconstruction of Ezekiel's life is that he was called to prophesy in Jerusalem in 593; that is, in the fifth year of King Jehoiachin's captivity, as 1: 2 says. At some point we cannot date exactly, though it was before the fall of the city in 586, Ezekiel left Jerusalem for one of the Judaean towns. This is connected with the symbolic act described in Chapter 12, where the prophet goes through the actions of one leaving his home in the semblance of an exile. Yahweh says to him: "Thou shalt remove from this place to another place in their sight" (12: 3). The other place is some unnamed town of Judaea. This residence in a Judaean town explains the statement that the news of the fall of Jerusalem was brought to the prophet by a fugitive (33: 21), *on that day* (24: 26), an impossibility if he were then in Babylon. It was not until shortly after the fall of Jerusalem in 586 that Ezekiel actually went into exile. This, it must be admitted, does not explain the enigmatic date with which the book opens: "in the thirtieth year". But no one has yet offered a satisfactory explanation of this date, which might be, as Bertholet himself suggests, a mistake for "in the thirteenth year", i.e. 585. Possibly, however, as Begrich argues, the date is an equation with the fifth year since there seems to have been a difference of twenty-five years in the chronology of Chronicles.

In support of this reconstruction, Bertholet can point to a number of details, as well as to the general probability that much of 1–24 would be spoken to, and done among, those whom it concerned, i.e. undoubtedly the people of Jerusalem and Judaea. In 5: 2 the prophet is told to burn part of the hair of his head and beard "in the midst of the city", which can hardly mean in the midst of the diagram of the city which he has drawn on a clay brick. In 11: 13, one of the leading idolaters, Pelatiah, is said to have died, in fulfilment of the prophet's denunciation, which might well have happened in real life; but how is such an event related to a vision and a visionary presence of the prophet? In 12: 9, the "rebellious house" of Israel asks him next morning after he has simulated going into exile: "What are you doing?" But the rebellious house clearly means the threatened Judaeans—how could they say this to him unless he was living among them? In v. 19 he refers to "the people of the land (i.e. Judaea). In 20: 31, we read: "When ye offer your gifts, when ye make your sons to pass through the fire, do ye pollute yourselves with all their idols, *unto this day*?" (cf. 14: 7). Such idolatry may easily be conceived as going on in Jerusalem and Judaea in reaction from the failure of the Josianic Reformation; but it can hardly be conceived as applying to the exiles in Babylon and as describing the contemporary state of Jewish religion there. In 33: 24, we hear of "the inhabitants of *these* waste places", which suggests that the speaker is himself on the spot, and not hundreds of miles away.

It would not be profitable to attempt any precise enumeration of the oracles which are Palestinian or Babylonian respectively, especially as doubt must remain in many instances. But, substantially, Chapters 1–24 contain Palestinian oracles, apart from the first chapter and a few scattered portions. Most of the foreign prophecies seem to have been written before 586, and therefore in Judaea; that against Ammon in Chapter 25 presupposes the fall of Jerusalem. The natural background of the prophecies of restoration which follow the foreign prophecies in the present arrangement will be the prophet's exile in Babylon; much of Chapters 33–42 can still be used to illustrate the exilic conditions. As for the closing part of the book (40–48) describing the future temple and its worship, Bertholet accepts much of this as Ezekiel's, whilst allowing, as we certainly must for considerable later expansion and addition, which such material would invite. Galling, who contributes to the archaeological discussion of this reconstruction, dismisses the theory that it was really a building plan for the actual second temple, and thinks it probable that the reconstruction dates from the early years of the exile and is from Ezekiel. On architectural grounds, he argues that the planner knew the temple both in its undestroyed and destroyed state, i.e. round about 586 (in Bertholet, p. xx).

If, then, we provisionally accept this latest theory of the composition of the book, the chief difference from the conventional view will be that we must interpret the earlier half with the background of Jerusalem and Judaea, and not of Babylon and the exiles, and that we have no need to raise difficult psychical theories as to Ezekiel's telepathy and clairvoyance. Just as we know that Jeremiah gathered up and reapplied his earlier prophecies over twenty years (36), so we may suppose that Ezekiel in Babylon gathered up his Judaean prophecies when in Babylon and gave them a new application. In any case, as indeed for all the prophets, we must allow for the possibility of later additions.

Our further study of the book falls into three natural divisions. The prophet himself concerns us first of all, especially because there are striking features in his prophetic consciousness which distinguish him from his fellows, features which by their fuller detail illuminate the nature of the prophetic consciousness in general. In fact, any study of that consciousness must be based on him and his older contemporary, Jeremiah; men so different, yet sharing a common purpose and interpreting history by similar principles, though in very different applications. In the second place we shall consider the characteristic features of the theology of Ezekiel, and here again we shall find that he is more consciously a theologian than any of his predecessors. In the third place, we shall consider his outlook on the future, under the heading of "Israel and the Nations". More explicitly than any of the other prophets he anticipates that which shall be in the generations to come. If he lacks the attractive breadth of his immediate successor, Deutero-Isaiah, he comes much closer to the actual course of events, a closeness which has won for him the well-known title, "the father of Judaism".

THE PROPHETIC CONSCIOUSNESS OF EZEKIEL

Whenever we possess an account of the call of a prophet, we naturally expect it to be a primary document for the understanding of the man and his message. For this experience must have been the supreme moment of his life. His human personality here encountered the divine in a specially intense contact, and revealed itself for what it was in the very moment of surrendering itself to something higher. Moreover, a prophetic call was not given in a vacuum; it was not an ordination to an undefined ministry. Hebrew realism required that the call should be closely linked to a particular occasion. So we generally find that political events bear some relation to the prophet's sense of vocation and sometimes seem to be its immediate stimulus, whilst his moral reaction to them and to their social content or accompaniments will also figure in the account of his call.

These general expectations we find fulfilled in one prophet after another, though in greater or less degree. Amos has told us little directly concerning his call, because his reference to it is only incidental, in self-defence against the taunt of the priest Amaziah. He simply says that he was "taken" from his sheep and sycamores to prophesy. But we can be sure that his experience of that taking included a real content, which may indeed be recorded for us in the five visions of destruction with which the book now closes. Hosea again carries back his prophetic consciousness to those circumstances and issues of his marriage which have left so clear an impress on the contents of his message. Isaiah reveals through the account of his call his own characteristic sense of the holiness of God and of the sinfulness of Israel's pride, which will refuse to listen to the message. Jeremiah not less characteristically shrinks from his task and has to be promised a strength not his own to achieve its impossibility.

1. *The Two Calls*

The prophet Ezekiel, who is our present concern, not only tells us of his call in much fuller detail than any other prophet, but apparently describes two distinct calls, however much this fact has been obscured by the editorial work which has run them together. As we saw in the last chapter, the account of the written roll, which the prophet eats, may refer to his initial call to prophesy in Jerusalem and Judaea, whilst the vision of the throne-chariot which now begins the book may be his second call to prophesy in Babylon after the fall of Jerusalem.

The account of the book-roll vision is found in 2: 3 to 3: 9. We notice at the outset that the statement of the prophet's message to "a rebellious house" is given in what appear to be two recensions of the same contents: 2: 3–7 and 3: 4–7. This putting together of different versions of the same thing is a constant feature of the Book of Ezekiel and is more likely to be due to the redactors than to the prophet himself. One of the versions (3: 8, 9) contains the prophet's self-portrait: "I have made thy face hard against their faces and thy forehead hard against their foreheads"; he is a stern and grim-faced prophet throughout; we ought to respect him, but we shall hardly love him. He is in no doubt from the very outset as to the reception of his words by Israel, but the words have to be spoken whether Israel listens or refuses to listen. A prophet is a necessary link in the chain of divine activity; he must speak before the judgment comes, even though to vindicate rather than to avert it.

The particular form of the visionary experience is highly characteristic. The prophet sees a hand stretched out to him, holding the roll and unrolling it to show that both its back and front are covered with dire words, words of lamentation and mourning and woe. This is the content of his future message. He is ordered to eat the roll, and when he takes it into his mouth he finds it sweet as honey (cf. Jer. 15: 16: "Thy words were found and I did eat them and thy words were unto me a joy"). The "sweetness" expresses the intrinsic attractiveness of the word of God and the inner joy of obedience to it, however bitter its contents. We may compare Ps. 119: 103:

> How sweet are thy words upon my palate!
> Yea, sweeter than honey to my mouth!

A further point to notice, as throwing light on Ezekiel's characteristics, is that the revelation comes to him as something written, rather than spoken. We are in the post-Deuteronomic age, when for the first time in the religion of Israel there had been public and general acceptance of a book as the basis of religion. With the fateful consequences of that change of emphasis, both for good and for evil, we are not here concerned. But it corresponds with the fact that the Book of Ezekiel is the most "literary" of any of the greater prophets. It contains more consciously verbal composition, more theoretical reflexion, than those of his predecessors, even if we allow for a large measure of editorial work of this kind as being incorporated in the book. There is more recognition of the word of God as something fixed and predetermined. We notice also that the contents of this roll are wholly denunciatory. This agrees with the first half of the book (1–24) for by far the greater part, and is a confirmation of the view that a second call was needed in the changed conditions of Babylon after the fall of Jerusalem to start the prophet forth on a new mission of hopeful reconstruction.

The second call, as we may name the opening chapter, following Bertholet, cannot be exactly dated, in spite of the first verse of the chapter.[1] "The thirtieth year" offers an enigma of which there is no satisfactory solution, because no one has yet found a date from which to reckon it. Bertholet himself thinks that it is due to a scribal error for "the thirteenth year", which might then be reckoned as from the first deportation in 597 and give us a date shortly after the destruction of Jerusalem. The essential features of the throne-chariot vision are that the prophet sees a storm-cloud from the north gradually differentiating itself into a chariot bearing a throne on which is the figure of Yahweh. The platform on which the throne rests is supported at its corners by four shapes, each with four heads, whilst the wheels of the chariot are able to move in any direction when it runs on the earth. In the air, motion is given by the wings of the four figures, who, as we infer from the parallel passage in Chapter 10, are really cherubim, the mythical figures associated with the storm-cloud, the supporters of the storm-god; we think of Psalm 18: 10:

> *He rode upon a cherub and did fly,*
> *Yea, he flew swiftly upon the wings of the wind.*

Unity of movement is given by the *ruach* or "spirit" which animates both the figures and the wheels, making an organism out of a mechanism. In the parallel description of Chapter 10, there seems to be an altar in the

[1] The complexity of 1: 1–3 is seen from the mingling of first and third persons, repetition of place and formulae of revelation, and the double dating.

midst of the figures, from which the blazing coals of fire are taken to be scattered upon the doomed city, like incendiary bombs. The central feature of this call-experience, as Bertholet emphasizes, is that God's chariot throne is *movable*; the throne is no longer established over Jerusalem as it was to the prophetic eyes of Isaiah. God has come to His prophet in far-off Babylon; He has left the city which is no longer worthy of His presence. This departure is described in 10: 18 ff., and the return to the future city to be built is seen in the vision of 43: 1–4.

It is easy to see in this highly complex vision the combination of many elements—e.g. the sapphire firmament of the vision of Moses and the elders on Sinai: "they saw the God of Israel; and there was under His feet as it were a paved work of sapphire stones" (Exod. 24: 10). Bertholet thinks that the great bronze lavers on wheels in the temple courts have helped to shape the prophet's mental picture; whilst the composite creatures of Mesopotamian architecture may also have had their influence on the four-headed figures, combining the eagle's speed, the lion's majesty, the ox's strength, and the man's reason—which is, as Bertholet says, an attempt to express the divine omniscience and omnipresence. We have always to remember that Hebrew ways of thinking had to turn our abstracts into material symbols, which accounts for much of the strangeness of apocalyptic. It is clear that in such a vision as this we are on the way to apocalyptic, even if Chapters 38 and 39 belong to a later period than that of Ezekiel.

2. *The Symbolic Acts*

A second very marked feature of the Book of Ezekiel is the large number of symbolic acts performed by the prophet. Such acts are by no means confined to him; they were part of the common form of prophecy. They are not to be regarded, as they often are, as simply Oriental gesticulation and dramatic physical movement accompanying speech. They are the direct descendants of the symbolic magic which we find all over the world, though in the hands of the prophets the magic becomes genuine religion since it is performed at the command of God, and is a form of His word to man. By the symbolic act the prophet felt that he was releasing the energies of God to accomplish God's purpose.

A number of such symbolic acts are collected in Chapters 4 and 5, all relating to the coming fate of Jerusalem and its people, though they may have belonged to different times. The prophet traces the outline of the city on a clay brick, and then builds up mimic siege works around it, which include the use of an iron griddle which he doubtless had handy. He himself, setting his face against it as a besieger, represents and enacts the divine purpose to reduce it. Then we read that he was to lie upon his left side to represent the period of punishment by exile for the northern kingdom, and upon his right side to represent that of the southern kingdom. We need not think that the act was necessarily continuous for the long period stated. The lying down might be accompanied by some token indication of the period it represented (if the numbers here are original). There follows a reference to siege-rations, scanty and rough, to be eaten once a day at a fixed time. People will have to eat what they can get, and not much of that, and the water is as scanty as the food. The fuel for baking is such as would horrify a strict Jew in normal times, since it would make the food technically "unclean". This may be a distinct symbolic act, as it is referred to the subsequent exile (13).

In Chapter 5, the prophet cuts off the hair of his head

and his beard and divides it into three parts to be variously destroyed or scattered, so representing the varying doom of the inhabitants of Jerusalem. If this procedure strikes us as peculiarly odd, we should remember that the hair was regarded as a special seat of life—hence the hair-offerings, and so could take the place of the life of the city with which the prophet is identified. As merely a dramatic illustration, the whole thing would be puerile enough; but as the way in which, through the prophet, Yahweh initiated the doom of the people, it has a new meaning.

To the same cycle of siege and downfall symbols belongs the detailed enactment of "going into exile", which we find in Chapter 12. This, like the others, we may place in Jerusalem shortly before the downfall. The prophet "packs up" for departure, as one who knows that he must carry on his own back all he takes. He digs a hole in the mud wall of his house and simulates escape in the dark by it. If we think about the meaning of this symbolic act, we shall see that it would have been futile if performed amongst people who had already gone into exile. Those of the 597 deportation already in Babylon knew the real thing and needed no prophet's act to bring it about. But those left in Jerusalem refused to believe that they would have to follow their fellow-countrymen. For them and to them, that is, in Jerusalem, the prophet must have done these things.

We may believe that the prophet's symbolic act was itself his real manner of departure from Jerusalem to go to some other place in Judaea. We often find an actual event made into a symbol, as we shall see with the death of the prophet's wife. It is as though he said: See what has happened to me; see also its meaning for you. The following symbol of food and water taken with trembling and anxiety may have been enacted in the place to which Ezekiel withdrew (so Bertholet, who stresses the reference to "the people of the land" (19), which could not refer to the exiles in Babylon; the whole description of the stricken land applies to Judaea, and implies that the prophet is himself there). A similar act is described in 21: 11, 12 (E.T. 6, 7), viz. sighing and groaning as of one who has received devastating news.

Finally, as a fitting close to this phase of the prophet's activity, we have the remarkable account of the death of his wife (24: 15–27), the only incident of private and domestic life to which he refers, and then only for prophetic purposes. We can imagine how differently Hosea would have reacted to the same event, whilst also seeing in it a divinely designed symbol. Both Ezekiel and Hosea, however, men of such differing temperaments, show us how objectively the prophetic consciousness functioned. They and their feelings were nothing; the word of Yahweh was everything and commandeered all of themselves that it could use. The point of this symbolic act is, however, not simply the death of Ezekiel's wife, though this offers a parallel to the people's loss of their sanctuary, but also the way in which he is to react to it. Every natural impulse to mourn, expressed visibly and audibly in Oriental fashion, is to be checked. There is no place for tears. So, the overwhelming catastrophe will stun men into silence, and, like the prophet, his fellow-countrymen will be dumb. The prophet arrests the attention of those about him by abstaining from the customary mourning for his wife—an abstinence which would be regarded as a shocking thing. We notice here, again, in spite of some later expansion of the theme, the fact that a fugitive from Jerusalem is said to bring the news of the fall of the city on the same day (25–26), a manifest impossibility if the prophet had not been in the near neighbourhood.

We have seen that these symbolic acts of Ezekiel,

varied as they are, are all concentrated on the fall of Jerusalem. That, with its interpretation, was the dominating event of his life, so that the concentration is natural enough. In the subsequent activity in Babylon, there is only one such act, and that is of a subordinate kind. It is found in 37: 15 ff., where the prophet writes the name of Judah on one stick and that of Israel on another, and joins them together, to signify the future reunion of the two parts of the people. But, as we shall see from point to point, there are allegories which may sometimes have been enacted, like the filled pot and the rusty pot of 24: 1–14, and visions of quasi-objective reality, like that of the valley of dry bones. It is not always possible to draw a sharp line of division between allegory and symbolic act.

The symbolic acts which we have reviewed are apt to suggest to us the "make-believe" of a child, which is perhaps the reason why some interpreters of Ezekiel have hesitated to regard them as more than figures of speech. But the prophets were able to enter their kingdom of the Spirit just because in some respects they were children, and could take their "make-believe" so seriously. Through these trivialities (as they seem to us) they were conscious of exerting power, not over Yahweh, but on His behalf over outer events, just as the child is conscious of power in its "make-believe". Indeed, we may say that the attraction of such play to the child is partly in the consciousness of such power. The child being necessarily excluded in some degree from the world of "grown-ups", creates a world of its own, intensely real, into which they can hardly enter, a world which he can control. It is not less difficult for us to enter into the world of the prophet, the world in which what we call solid realities could crumble or be transformed at the touch of God, whilst His word endured for ever.

3. *The Hand and the Spirit of Yahweh*

There are other features in the behaviour and prophetic consciousness of Ezekiel, besides the frequency of his resort to acted symbolism, which single him out from other prophets. We notice his more frequent use of the phrase "the hand of Yahweh" to denote divine control, together with his use of the term *ruach*, which the greater prophets seem to avoid; whilst there is also evidence for *alalia* (temporary dumbness) and catalepsy, if not also of telepathy and clairvoyance, as the conventional view requires. "The hand of Yahweh" is described as coming upon Ezekiel at the time of the throne-chariot vision (1: 3), and again at the renewal of the vision after seven days of stupor (3: 22). In 592–591, a year after his first call, we read (8: 1): "as I was sitting in my house, with the elders of Judah sitting before me, the hand of the Lord Yahweh fell upon me there"; with the result that ecstasy (in the proper sense of the word) seizes him, for he is taken by a lock of his hair and carried "in visions of God" to Jerusalem to see its idolatry. When the fugitive reached him with the news that the city had fallen (33: 22), he had experienced the hand of Yahweh on the previous evening, but the release from dumbness came only with the arrival of the fugitive. The hand of Yahweh came upon him to lead him into the vision of the valley of dry bones (37: 1), and also into those of the reconstructed city and temple (40: 1). It is clear that the phrase points to some abnormal state of consciousness.

In the use of the important term *ruach*, also, Ezekiel shows exceptional features; and offers, indeed, a landmark in the history of the term. The book employs it fifty-two times in all, i.e. about one-seventh of the 378 cases in the Old Testament. In twelve of these it is simply "wind" [1] (1: 4; 5: 2; 13: 11, 13; 17: 10; 19: 12; 27: 26; 37: 9, 9, 9, 10, 14), though we must not forget that the wind itself was quasi-supernatural, a divine energy. Hence, the word can be used of a supernatural power taking psychical instead of physical form; did not the panting of an excited man suggest that *ruach* energy had taken possession of him? So the wind that blows through the valley of dry bones is a quasi-supernatural wind able to impart life to the dead, and to become their "breath", the life-principle (37: 5); "I am causing *ruach* to enter into you, so that you live" (so vv. 6, 8). [2] Here we see *ruach* as supernatural power from without becoming the equivalent of the usual term for "breath" (*neshamah*), and *for the first time*. I know of no earlier instance in the Old Testament, though the term subsequently becomes a higher synonym for "soul" as the human "spirit". It is worth asking whether Ezekiel's marked "supernaturalism" may not have led to this acclimatization within human personality. In this connection, we notice that the term occurs five times of the "new *ruach*" which Yahweh will give to the Israel of the future (11: 19; 18: 31; 36: 26, 27; 39: 29), exactly the usage which might have led to the later psychical use of the term. [3]

Of the prophetic consciousness itself, *ruach* is used eleven times in the book, a remarkable number when we remember that the greater prophets seem to avoid the term as applied to their own inspiration. When Ezekiel was prostrate before the throne-chariot of his vision, *ruach* entered into him enabling him to stand on his feet (2:

[1] The derivative use of *ruach* (ten instances) to denote "quarter" or "region" need not concern us (e.g. 37: 9; 42: 16).

[2] 21: 12 (E.T. v. 7) shows the opposite, viz. lifelessness.

[3] Examples of this occur in 20: 32: "that which comes up upon your *ruach*"; and 11: 5, instead of the usual phrase "upon your heart" (14: 3, 7; 38: 10).

2; cf. 3: 24); *ruach* afterwards lifted him up and carried him to the exiles (3: 12, 14), as, in the present framework of the Jerusalem trance, *ruach* transfers him in vision to Jerusalem and the temple (8: 3), or from one part of the temple to another (11: 1) and brings him back (11: 24) [the second occurrence (*beruach*) is doubtful]. The *ruach* of Yahweh falls upon him to enable him to denounce the idolaters (11: 5). He was carried out by *ruach* to the valley of dry bones (37: 1). In the final vision of the return of Yahweh to Jerusalem, *ruach* brings him into the inner court (43: 5).

To this remarkable emphasis on *ruach* as the supernatural source of energy we must add the peculiar non-personal, or at least non-human, usage of *ruach* in the throne-chariot vision. Here it is the immanent energy giving unity to the figures and the wheels (1: 12, 20, 20, 20, 21; 10: 17). Ezekiel might be called *par excellence*, the prophet of *ruach*, and that *ruach* energy found visible expression. He is described as smiting his thigh and stamping his feet (6: 11; 21: 14, 17). Some of the symbolic acts which he was inspired to perform involved considerable physical energy, such as the brandishing of a sword (21: 9 ff.).

The question has been raised whether Ezekiel's condition was at least intermittently pathological; whether the motionless position he assumed was really a sort of catalepsy and the loss of speech was due to physical causes, though interpreted by the prophet as due to the divine command.[1] There is no reason why this should not have been the way in which Ezekiel made his contact with God; faith's power to interpret and so trans-

[1] 3: 25, 26. "I will place cords upon you, and I will make your tongue cleave to your palate." In this connection, we may note that the loss of speech may conceivably explain the increase in the resort to symbolic acts—prophetic "dumb-show". These follow the reference (3: 26) to the dumbness.

form affliction is one of its most cherished faculties. The point is of interest to us psychologically, rather than religiously. We have already seen that the transference of the prophet's earlier work to Jerusalem and Judaea lessens the demand for abnormal powers such as telepathy and clairvoyance. In any case, Ezekiel remains a strange and rather bewildering personality, and not least because of the great contrast between the earlier and later phases of his work.

4. *The Prophet and the Priest*

We saw in the first lecture that the crucial question for literary criticism concerned the immediate background of the prophet's work—was it Babylon or Judaea or both?—and we decided that it was both. Here our problem is a different one—how to reconcile two differing thought-worlds. Up to 586 the date of the fall of Jerusalem, we find a single-minded denunciation and threat of coming judgment; after it, we have prophecies of restoration and elaborate plans of reconstruction. There is, of course, no difficulty in supposing that Ezekiel should turn to the future of Israel and declare God's purpose to restore it, as he had previously declared God's purpose to destroy it. The temple vision is dated 573, i.e. thirteen years after the fall of Jerusalem, which allows time for the development of a changed outlook in Ezekiel. The difficulty is rather in regard to the way in which we pass, in the closing chapters, from the prophetic to the priestly interest. We find there much material which would be natural in the Book of Leviticus, but is hardly what we should expect from a prophet: the detailed measurements of the new temple (40–42); the regulations for its worship (43–46); the geographical division of the land (47–48). We hardly meet this difficulty by remembering that Ezekiel is described as priest, as well as prophet, in the opening verses; or, at any rate, as the son of a priest.[1] We have to account for what seems a complete change of emphasis—how and why the prophet should revert to priestly interests in this manner. The degree of difficulty can be diminished by supposing, as most commentators now do, that these chapters have been considerably expanded, in the same way as the ritual elements in the Pentateuch (for a division of the Ezekiel elements and the later additions on conservative lines, see G. A. Cooke, pp. 427-8). But, even to retain the framework of temple reconstruction for Ezekiel, requires us to see in him somewhat of a dual personality.

Perhaps, in view of the peculiar features already noticed in this prophet, that is a proper admission. In the reconstruction of other people's experience, especially in ancient times, we are always tending to over-simplification. We forget that they were men in many respects of like passions with ourselves, and that our own visible acts and final decisions have behind them a mass of inconsistent thoughts and feelings which never see the light. Sometimes circumstances bring out these diverse elements in surprising ways. Mr. Aldous Huxley, in *Grey Eminence*, his brilliant study of Father Joseph, the power behind the throne of Cardinal Richelieu, has shown us such a dual personality. We see a man rigorous in his practice of mystical religion, on the one hand; and, at the same time, the shrewd and unscrupulous politician, ready to get power at any price. Richelieu himself had two nicknames for his colleague, describing these two sides of him. One was "Tenebroso-Cavernoso" for the politician; the other, for the Franciscan evangelist and mystic was—"Ezéchiely"! Of course, the duality in Ezekiel was of a very different kind from that in Father Joseph; for

[1] Note also his ritual zeal in 4: 14 (nothing unclean).

Ezekiel was wholly a man of religion, whether as priest or prophet. The most likely theory would be that Ezekiel's intensity in denunciation passed into equal intensity in reconstructing the future. The catastrophe of 586, for such a man, is probably enough to explain the transition from the earlier to the later phase of his prophetic consciousness, so that it is not so strange that he should offer us a prophetic parallel to the priestly-prophetic compromise of the Book of Deuteronomy.

We may fittingly close this review of Ezekiel's prophetic consciousness by quoting the interesting passage in which he pictures himself as delivering the message. It is not certain whether this should be referred to the Judaean or to the Babylonian period (33: 30–33):

> As for you, O mortal man, your fellow-countrymen who talk of you by the walls and at the doors of the houses say to one another, "Come and hear what the word is that comes from Yahweh!" They come to you as my people used to come; and they sit before you, as if they were still my people: they listen to your words, but they will not obey them; for with their mouths they make a show of love, but their minds are set upon their own selfish gain. You are to them like a singer of love songs, with a beautiful voice, and able to play well on the instrument; they listen to your words, but they will not obey them. Only when the hour comes—and it is coming—they shall know that a prophet has been in the midst of them.

The final sentence points clearly to the essential place of the prophet. If "the prophet's function is to interpret history in the light of God's purpose for His people"[1] the prophet's vindication must come from history itself.

[1] G. A. Cooke, p. 369.

THE THEOLOGY OF EZEKIEL

Every human consciousness, however circumscribed and tarnished, is a mirror of the divine. The prophet of God is a man who has had the reflecting surface of his consciousness cleansed by the hand of God. But the quality of the image, dim or clear, crooked or true, is always conditioned by the scope and angle of the mirror. We cannot mistake Ezekiel's image of God for that of Hosea or Jeremiah; the temperaments of the men are too different. The true picture of God is not that of a composite photograph in which all the particular prophetic images are merged into a rather blurred and featureless presentment. The truth consists in the difference as well as in the resemblances.

A now-forgotten poetess of the Victorian age—Barbara Miller—wrote an impressive poem on Ezekiel's reaction to his wife's death in which she has credited him with what might have been Jeremiah's:

> *I dare not mourn*
> *The while I speak His word, for no weak tears*
> *May fall upon the sacred fire; no sound*
> *Of breaking human heart may mar the full*
> *Majestic music of a Prophet's voice.*

The attribution of such sensitiveness to the prophet makes him more human and therefore more attractive to us. But I cannot conceive Ezekiel as feeling sorrow in the same way as his more sensitive contemporary, much less as revealing the struggle within him. Ezekiel was a proud and stern man; proud because God had singled him out to be His watchman; stern because he was disgusted and angry with the world about him. Ezekiel's God also is proud and stern; proud of His name, stern in His retribution; though this is not, as we shall see, the whole of the story.

1. *The Honour of God*

Perhaps the most salient feature in Ezekiel's conception of God is the *honour* of God, both in the objective sense of the transcendent majesty of the divine, and in the subjective sense of God's concern that His Name be not dishonoured. In the former, Ezekiel continues Isaiah's emphasis on the holiness of God; and it is with Isaiah that Ezekiel has here most affinity. But Isaiah's God, for all His holiness, is more closely linked to man than is Ezekiel's; He is the Holy One of Israel, who dwells in Jerusalem. Ezekiel, as we have seen, detaches Yahweh from the holy city now profane, and gives Him a movable throne. The God whom Isaiah saw above the temple, majestic and holy as He is, is still a more human figure than we saw in the strange complex of the throne-chariot. Isaiah, from the outset, is sustained by faith in the unseen, and characteristically demands such faith from men. Ezekiel, assimilating the written roll, demands obedience, rather than faith, and frames the formal requirements of God more explicitly than any other prophet before or after him. Characteristically, his name for Israel is "rebellious", i.e. "disobedient" house.

The peculiar emphasis of Ezekiel on God's sense of His own honour comes out in the references to the Name of God, as in the fourfold repetition of the refrain "I wrought for My name's sake" in the historical review of Chapter 20. Here we must not do Ezekiel the injustice of supposing that he means "name" in the modern sense, as though God were merely concerned for His reputation, which is always a sign of weakness. (How careless Jesus

96

was of His "name" in our sense!) "Name" in the Bible often means "Nature"; the inner personality brought into outer manifestation and expression. We forget that "Christian name" was once supposed to be the expression of a new personality, changed by grace. In the Old Testament, the Name of God is Himself in action; as when Isaiah says: "Behold, the name of Yahweh cometh from far, burning in His anger" (30: 27). As Pedersen puts it, in his valuable study of the meaning of "Name" (*Israel* I–II, p. 248): "The outward reputation cannot be separated from the inner value." Consequently, Yahweh's appeal to His name is an appeal to His nature, His essential being. This comes out in the historical review which has already been mentioned (20). In verse 9, it is for His name's sake, because He is what He is, that Yahweh delivers Israel from Egypt. In verse 14, He does not destroy them in the desert, as they deserve through their disobedience, for His name's sake; and, similarly, in verse 22. The closing verse of the review (44) is:

> And you shall know that I am Yahweh, when I have dealt with you for my name's sake and not in accordance with your evil ways and your corrupt doings.

Thus it is the grace of God as well as His justified indignation and wrath which springs from His name. This comes out also in the great passage to be found in Chapter 36 (21 ff.): "I was grieved for My holy name which the house of Israel had caused to be profaned among the nations to which they came. . . . It is not for your sake that I am about to act, O house of Israel, but for My holy name. . . . I will restore the holiness of My great name." Then follows the promise of regenerating grace, which will concern us later.

The frequent references to the "jealousy" of God, in Ezekiel as elsewhere in the Old Testament, are to be understood with a similar difference of meaning. The Hebrew word (*kin'ah*) originally denoting the hot flush of emotion (Arabic *kana'*, dye red) can indeed mean "jealousy", in our sense, such as a husband's towards a wife (Prov. 6: 34), but it also means "zeal" and noble passion, such as that which men feel for the house of God (Ps. 99: 9), or such as God feels for His people:

> *Where are Thy zeal and Thy might,*
> *Thy yearning pity and mercy?*
>
> (Isa. 63: 15.)

Ezekiel frequently uses it of God's righteous anger against men, the zeal of His indignation against Israelite faithlessness (23: 25), or against Gentile oppression of Israel (35: 11; 36: 6). "Jealousy" is a misleading rendering for this proper indignation of the righteous God against all unrighteousness, issuing in that divine judgment which the kingly rule of God demands.

The limitations in Ezekiel's conception of God are not, therefore, to be sought in his insistence on God's honour and its vindication, for every true prophet must insist on that, but in the manner of its fulfilment. We must not expect to find in Him even such foreshadowings of the Gospel of the Cross as we get in Hosea, that

> *authentic sign and seal*
> *Of Godship, that it ever waxes glad,*
> *And more glad, until gladness blossoms, bursts*
> *Into a rage to suffer for mankind.*
>
> (*Balaustion's Adventure*, p. 654.)

Ezekiel belongs to the order of John the Baptist, and in this aspect he that is least in the kingdom of heaven is greater than he. But there can be no adequate understanding of the Christian Gospel which does not incorporate the demand for the honour of God in righteous judgment. Nor must we forget that it is to Ezekiel we owe the familiar words (33: 11): "I have no pleasure in the death of the wicked; but that the wicked turn from his way and live."

2. *The Sin of Idolatry*

This brings us to the second point in the characteristic theology of Ezekiel, viz. the wickedness of his contemporaries which he is attacking. There can be no doubt as to what he puts in the forefront of this. That which most of all wrongs the honour of God is the idolatry which replaces Him by other gods. This is most apparent in the description of alien cults observed in the temple of Yahweh in Ezekiel's own times, the description given in Chapter 8. Here there are four kinds of idolatry in view, besides a fifth "abomination" which it is not easy to identify.

The first offence is the presence of what is called in our versions "the image of jealousy" at or near the north gate of the temple (3). The word for "image" (*semel*), regarded as "statue", is usually identified with that which Manasseh placed in the temple (2 Chron. 33: 7, 15). This is further identified in 2 Kings 21: 7, with "the graven image (*pesel*) of the *ashera*" (cf. Deut. 4: 16). The *ashera* frequently denotes a sacred tree or wooden post, but sometimes, as here, it refers to a goddess Ashera, a consort of Baal (Albright, *Archaeology and the Religion of Israel*, p. 78). Professor Albright, however, has recently given reasons for regarding the object as a figured slab set in the wall (*ibid.*, p. 165 and note). This would conform to Syro-Assyrian practice, for which there is plenty of archaeological evidence. The description of it as the "image" or "slab" of jealousy, means that which arouses the indignation of Yahweh, whose rights are infringed by its presence.

The second instance of idolatry is that of a room whose walls are cut with the figures of reptiles and beasts "and all the idols of the House of Israel" (v. 10). Before these, seventy elders are burning incense. The use of incense is first mentioned, and with disapproval, by Jeremiah (6: 20). The animal figures suggest Egyptian cults, and the practice may be influenced by the resort of a pro-Egyptian political party to Egypt for aid against Babylonia. The worshippers defend this secret practice of theirs by saying that Yahweh has left the land, and therefore cannot see it.

The third instance is found near the northern gate, where women are weeping for Tammuz. This is definitely the Babylonian cult which can be traced back to 3000 B.C., so that it can claim to be one of the oldest forms of religious worship in the world (Cooke). This ritual mourning is for the drying-up of the spring vegetation by the summer heat and is carried out in terms of the mythology which made Tammuz, the Phoenician Adon and the Greek Adonis, into the dying lover of Ishtar, annually raised to new life. The Babylonian form of the cult may have been a recent importation into Palestine (Albright, p. 167), or was a revival of Ras Shama (Canaanite) mythology.

The fourth instance is that of twenty-five men between the porch and the great altar, engaged in sun-worship, and consequently having their backs to the temple, in a sort of "black mass". There are many other traces of sun-worship amongst the Israelites. It will be remembered that the Code of Hammurabi is prefaced by the picture of the king before the seated sun-god, Shamash.

These particular instances, so graphically described by Ezekiel, are confirmed by his more general references. Thus, in the review of Israel's history in Chapter 20, Israel is accused of practising idolatry even in Egypt (7, 8); they continued their false devotion even in the desert (16), and found new forms of it in their future home (28):

> When I brought them to the land that I had sworn by uplifted hand to give to them, as often as they saw any high hill or any leafy tree, there they offered their sacrifices, and there they presented their offensive gifts; there they set forth their soothing odours and there they poured their libations.

It is perhaps difficult for us to enter into the full meaning of the prophetical denunciations of idolatry, just because we tend to think of it as a superstitious form of religion at a lower level than our own, but still sincere religion. But this is not what the prophets saw. They rightly regarded this assimilation of Israel's worship to that of the surrounding peoples as the abandonment of Israel's peculiar prerogative; in fact, Ezekiel here represents the people as saying (32): "We will be like the nations, the races of the lands, in serving wood and stone." The fertility cults in particular were accompanied by sexual practices which were alien to that nomadic strain of religion which the prophets so obviously continue. From our more modern standpoint, we may say that the vice of all forms of idolatry is that it fossilizes religion by fixing it to the static and material, whilst a prophetic religion is always dynamic and spiritual and able to adjust itself, even unconsciously, to new needs. The future of Yahwism lay with its rejection of idolatry, for that left it open to spiritual and ethical development.

But though Ezekiel helped to save Israel from the externalization of its religion in the form of idolatry, his general view of sin does not escape criticism from another standpoint. If we look at the list of sins denounced in Chapter 18, we find, indeed, the high social morality demanded by all the great prophets; the justice and the mercy which are the higher life of a nation. But the weakness here is that these are coupled with purely ritual demands, such as eating no flesh with the blood in it. You cannot put ritual and moral demands on the same level without tending to assimilate their value which means, for most people, the externalization of the moral demands into an outward obedience at the most; and, for some people, the exaltation of the ritual into something of intrinsic worth. We see the same danger in Chapter 22, where sins of sexual immorality and the oppression of the helpless through bribery are linked with the purely ritual breach or neglect of sabbath-observance (8). Some of the admitted weaknesses of later Judaism (as also of Christianity) can be already seen in Ezekiel's failure to discriminate in the evils he denounces.

3. *Individual Retribution*

How, then, does Ezekiel conceive that God deals with the foremost sin of idolatry in particular, and with other sins in general? Here we encounter one of the most characteristic of Ezekiel's contributions to theology, his individualism, which is set out in Chapter 18. To understand it, we must remember the two presuppositions which underlie it; the first, shared by the prophet with his people; the second, that of the people against which he is protesting. In the first place, neither the prophet nor his hearers have any knowledge of a life after death. The picture of Sheol given in Chapter 32 shows us a great international assembly of those who have lost anything that can be called "life". Their ancient distinctions of race and rank remain, but what is that to these ghosts, these shades? In particular, there is no exercise of moral discrimination amongst them; no opportunity, therefore, for retribution to be deferred beyond this life on earth.

Consequently, if evil is to be punished, it must be punished here and now.

The second presupposition is that of the people in general. Hitherto, the principle of corporate personality has ruled men's thoughts. Each man is bound up in the bundle of life with other men so that both law and religion treat the group as a unit. The individual may inculpate the group, as Achan did his whole family; Yahweh Himself visits the sins of the fathers "upon the children and upon the children's children, upon the third and upon the fourth generation" (Exod. 34: 7). Consequently the popular saying which Ezekiel, like Jeremiah before him (31: 29), here quotes, is quite orthodox:

> *The fathers eat sour grapes,*
> *The children's teeth are set on edge.*

Jeremiah had referred to it incidentally in introducing the prophecy of the new covenant, the individualism of which would cancel the old corporate interdependence. Ezekiel challenges it directly and in detail in order to meet the growing consciousness that it entailed injustice on the part of God, a consciousness reinforced by the mass-sufferings of deportation. The prophet is not formulating a new doctrine for its own sake; as is usual with the prophets, he is meeting an actual situation. He does this by a flat denial of the ancient doctrine of corporate responsibility before God.

Ezekiel traces an imaginary family history, through father, son, and grandson. The father is a good man, by all the standards which the prophet names. Very well, then; God is just and will surely give him life; that is, long life upon the earth. But he has an evil son, who, on the current doctrine, might have been covered from the wrath of God by his father's goodness. Not at all, says the prophet: God will deal with him in complete detachment from his father, and he will die; that is, a sudden judgment of God will fall on him. But *his* son may react from his father's evil ways into goodness again. Will he be condemned for his father's evil? Not at all, once more says the prophet: he will be rewarded like his grandfather (not because of his grandfather) with long life. This is the prophet's defence of God against the charge that God is unjust, and it is exactly the view which the friends of Job maintained. The principle of individual retribution may be true, but it is not the only truth, and men's lives cannot be treated as isolated units, any more than they can be wholly absorbed into a corporate personality. As so often, the too vigorous denial of one error leads to another.

The prophet then goes on to consider the relation of a man to his own past, instead of that of his ancestors. What happens if the wicked man repent? Ezekiel's answer is that the past is wiped out as completely as was his father's. The same thing happens to the good man, who turns to evil; his past of good is also forgotten, and God deals with him in his present attitude. How then, the prophet asks, can you accuse God of any injustice? The chapter concludes with a challenge to repent, and put God to the proof.

Here, again, we have to recognize the mingling of truth and error in the prophet's words. We do not want to minimize in the least the stress which he puts on repentance; that has the highest confirmation. The way a man is facing is the most important thing about him, and he ought to be judged by that, in the light of his potentialities, and not simply of an irrevocable past. But can he, even by a genuine repentance, altogether escape from that past? This is not the way in which he is treated by the law which society finds necessary for its preservation, and it is simply not true to psychology. There is an outer social handicap, an inner stain or inhibition, which evil generates, and they cannot be detached wholly from the sentence of God. Ezekiel's psychology is much too atomic to be true to life. Repentance itself must have a history.

These limitations in the prophet's contribution must be recognized, in order that we may fairly assess his great and necessary contribution to the truth of God's dealings with men. Revelation, like life, is much more complex than we are apt to think. Truth is not something that can be neatly packed into a formula. It comes out in the complex give and take of life, and it often takes more than one voice to utter the whole truth.

It is in harmony with the prophet's insistence on the individuality of God's relation to men that he himself is conscious of standing in a more individual relation to his fellow-Israelites than were his prophetic predecessors. This comes out in the new title which he claims, that of "watchman" (*zopheh*). As appears from 3: 16–21, and especially 33: 1–20, the point of the title is the responsibility which it entails. The watchman is appointed to give warning, but he cannot be held responsible for what people do with his warning. If he fails to give it, he is rightly held guilty; if he gives it, his responsibility is over. The statement is true, yet we note again a certain externality and detachment in the prophet, which does not rise into the fullest pastoral relation. Where that higher level is reached, the prophet cries: "But now, if Thou wilt forgive their sin . . . but if not, blot me out of Thy book which Thou hast written" (Exod. 32: 32) and the apostle echoes him: "I could wish that I myself were anathema from Christ for my brethren's sake, my kinsmen according to the flesh" (Rom. 9: 3).

4. *Regeneration*

The fourth noteworthy feature in the theology of

Ezekiel is his doctrine of regeneration. Here we must distinguish what he says about the renewal of the nation from that of the individual, and admit that these are not systematically co-ordinated. His most direct statement about the renewal of the nation is found in one of the best-known passages of the book, the vision of the valley of dry bones in Chapter 37. In the lonely valley to which he has been transported by divine control, he sees an ancient battlefield, for these are the bones of slain men (9). They are very dry; that is, all the life, psychical as well as physical, which Hebrew psychology ascribes to the bones, has long since left them. But some vestige of the ancient conception remains in the fact that the bones are addressed at God's command, and are enabled to respond. The stages of renewal are described in detail in accordance with Hebrew ideas of anatomy. First, there is the sound of the reassembly of the bones; bone to its bone—surely the most weird of all the sounds heard by prophetic ear. Then the sinews are put upon them, and the flesh is brought up upon these; and, last, the skin is spread over all; the distinction of the skin from the flesh reminds us of the darker Oriental colouring. But they are still dead men, though now men, for the animating principle of life, the breath, is not in them. Then the *ruach*, the supernatural wind that is itself both psychical and physical, blows into them from the four quarters of the earth, and they come alive and stand upon their feet, a very great army.

That is the vision, and there follows a clear statement of its meaning. The exiles had said, in what perhaps was a proverbial saying: "Our bones are dried up and our hope has perished; we are wholly cut off." Such a saying may well be the psychological nucleus of the prophet's vision, which is, as so often in the prophecies of Ezekiel, a denial of the current thought. The vision asserts that all things are possible with God, and that out of the very grave He can raise the dead. This does not mean that men then believed in a resurrection; it means just the opposite, since resurrection would be a miracle against all expectation. But the miracle in the vision is an enacted symbol of what will happen to the nation. From the grave of exile God will raise it up, and give it new life through His *ruach*, to resettle it in its own land.

The companion passage in the previous chapter (36) describes an inward renewal (16 ff.). The exilic dispersions were a penalty for sin, but they have been misinterpreted by the nations to which Israelites were exiled, and Yahweh's honour has suffered. So, not for Israel's sake, but for His name's sake, Yahweh will resanctify the dishonoured name.

> I will take you out of the nations and gather you from all the lands; and I will bring you to your own land. I will throw pure water over you and you shall be pure: from all your impurities; and from all your idolatries will I purify you. I will give you a new heart and will put within you a new spirit; I will remove the heart of stone out of your flesh and will give you a heart of flesh; and I will put my spirit within you and make you follow my statutes and be careful to observe my ordinances.
>
> (vv. 24–28.)

This great passage is Ezekiel's parallel to Jeremiah's prophecy of the New Covenant. Here, however, the figure used is that of a lustration or ceremonial washing, so widespread amongst the religions of the world. The Old Testament use of water in ceremonial cleansing passed to the baptism of proselytes, and so into the New Testament baptism. That which the outer symbol sets forth is an inner change of heart; that is, in the Hebrew idiom, a change of purpose. It is significant that the prophet regards such a regeneration, a new birth in the Johannine terminology, as essential to any future which is to be better than the past. The change of purpose will be seen in obedience to the commands of God. The old heart of stone was deaf and unresponsive to those commands and "petrified" in its wilfulness; the new heart of flesh will be responsive to the grace of God in His ample provision for the future:

> Then shall you remember your evil ways, and your doings that were not good; and you shall loathe yourselves for your sinful and abominable deeds.
>
> (v. 31.)

This discovery of the past sin of ingratitude due to divine grace is one of the deeper elements in Ezekiel's teaching. It is found in other places also, as in the allegory of the faithless wife (16: 61, 63; cf. 20: 43). It is probably the greatest of all evangelical motives, for the real discovery of what sin is must always be inseparable from the knowledge of grace.

The hope of this change, or rather the demand for it, is one aspect of Ezekiel's supernaturalism, of which mention has been made previously. But we must not unduly externalize this. Ezekiel has indeed said no more than to ascribe it to the spirit of God. But in 18: 31 he calls for repentance, i.e., conversion, which is the other side of regeneration:

> Repent, then, and turn from all your transgressions, lest your iniquity bring you to ruin. Cast away from you all the transgressions which you have committed against Me, and get yourselves a new heart and a new spirit.

There will always be these two aspects, the Godward and the manward, in any of the spiritual contacts of God with man. It will always be open to men to trace the psychological features and leave out of account their theological factors, or to ignore the human conditions and assert unintelligible miracle. The instructed servant of God will combine both elements, and interpret the psychology as the visible working-out of the theology.

It was Francis W. Newman, the Unitarian brother of John Henry, who first drew the distinction in Christian experience between the once-born and the twice-born, a distinction which William James brought into circulation. Ezekiel belongs beyond question to the twice-born line, the line of Saint Paul, Saint Augustine and Luther. Newman defines the once-born type as those "who no more shrink from God, than a child from an emperor before whom the parent trembles: for in fact they have no vivid conception of *any* of the qualities in which the severer Majesty of God consists". It is that severer Majesty which the theology of Ezekiel sets forth, and his theology, like that of the Bible in general, is of the twice-born type.

ISRAEL AND THE NATIONS

Some of Ezekiel's allegories alienate modern taste by their excessive realism, but there is one, less known than it ought to be, of great aesthetic appeal, because of its simplicity and restraint. This is the allegory of the wild vine in Chapter 15. The figure is familiar enough. [1] Palestine was a land of vines (Deut. 8: 8), and Jeremiah, in a prophecy of future restoration, says (31: 5):

> Once more shall ye plant your vineyards
> On the hills of Samaria.

Isaiah, in a famous parable, repeated and reapplied by a greater than he, had sung the song of Israel and Judah as Yahweh's vineyard (5). But Ezekiel is not thinking of the cultivated vine, cared for and protected in every way, as was Isaiah. He has gone back to the forest, the native home of the wild vine.

Ezekiel's poem bids us think of the vine in itself, apart from its fruit. Jotham's ancient fable of the trees had made the vine say: "Shall I refrain from my juice which gladdens gods and men?" for the grape is the one justification of the vine-tree. If it fails to produce grapes, it fails indeed, for its wood is good for nothing, and here other trees far eclipse it. Such is Israel, Ezekiel declares. Like its national emblem, it can be a tree of the choicest fruit; but, if it fail in this, it falls far short of other nations and is fit only for destruction, that destruction which he foresees in the coming fall of Jerusalem. Here

[1] The vine figures on coins of the First and Second Revolts.

is the little poem, relieved of some glosses which obscure its beauty:

> What shall be the wood of the vine
> More than all the wood of forest trees?
> Shall wood be taken from it to use for work?
> Shall they make from it a peg on which to hang anything?
> Lo, to the fire it is given for destruction,
> Its two ends the fire destroys
> And its middle is burnt; is it fit for service?
> Lo, when it was complete: it could serve for nothing,
> Much less, when fire has consumed it, is it fit for service.

1. The Judgment of Israel

The poem, written in Palestine not long before 586, expresses Ezekiel's consistently maintained attitude towards Jerusalem. The two long and laborious allegories in which he interprets the history of the past, those of the faithless wife in Chapter 16, and the two sisters in Chapter 23, give his justification for this coming judgment. In the former, we can see the influence of Hosea, the first to introduce this figure of Israel's infidelity. With relentless detail, the prophet describes the foundling on whom Yahweh took pity, the foundling whose father was an Amorite and whose mother was a Hittite. Through the divine pity, the outcast was cared for, and grew to adolescence, and Yahweh made her His bride, bestowing upon her every adornment. But she played him false with strangers and has amply deserved the fate that is coming upon her at their very hands. Judah, indeed, has behaved worse than her sister, Samaria. The allegory of the two sisters in Chapter 23 follows the same lines of realistic description, and the prophet spares us nothing in his detail. Samaria's name is Oholah and Judah's is Oholibah, both of them with scornful reference to the "tent" of prostitution (*ohel*). Judah is to drink the cup of judgment which Samaria has already drunk (v. 31).

The most direct announcements of the fall of Jerusalem may be seen in the sword-prophecies of Chapter 21, probably accompanied by the symbolic act of a brandished sword. The coming slaughter will be indiscriminate, as such disasters always are: "Thus saith Yahweh, Behold I am against you and I will draw My sword from its sheath, and will cut off from you righteous and wicked alike" (21: 3). The text is obscure and often corrupt, but we may think of the prophet brandishing a sword and crying out something of this kind (vv. 9 ff.):

> Sword! Sword! Sharpened and burnished. . . .
> Given to the slayer to grasp in his hand,
> Cry and howl, O mortal man
> For it has come upon my people
> Upon all the princes of Israel;
> Flung to the sword are they among my people.
> Smite upon thy thigh
> Let the sword be doubled, trebled.
> Sword of the slain is it,
> The great sword of the slain.

G. A. Cooke is justified in comparing it with the exultant paganism of Siegfried's Song at the forging of the sword (*Siegfried*, I, 3). The prophet is too much on the side of the executants of God's judgments to show any of the sympathy with the slain which Jeremiah so largely displays.

2. *The Judgment on the Nations*

On the other hand, the "foreign prophecies" of Chapters 25–32 proclaim a judgment on surrounding nations because of their attitude and conduct towards

Judah. This has its parallel in Isaiah, who recognizes the hand of Yahweh in the dealings of Assyria up to a point, but proclaims judgment on Assyria for passing beyond that point. We have a similar problem to face when we try to weigh and compare the good and the evil following from any historic event such as the World War: seldom is the issue one beyond dispute. So, in these chapters, the prophet turns altogether away from the judgment upon Israel which these nations helped to carry out, or at least approved, to what they themselves deserve for their treatment of Israel. Thus, to Ammon, which had been instigated to harass Jehoiakim when he rebelled against Nebuchadrezzar[1] (2 Kings 24: 2) Ezekiel says: "Because you cried 'Aha' over my sanctuary when it was profaned . . . I am handing you over to the Kedemites" (25: 3). For Moab, he proclaims the same fate. Moab had said: "Behold the house of Judah has become like other nations" (25: 8). Vengeance upon Edom for *their* vindictiveness will be executed by Israel herself (25: 14), perhaps because there was peculiar and often expressed bitterness against this people, as in the terrible curse of Psalm 137. This may account for the further prophecy against Edom in 35: 1–15, now placed as an introduction to Israel's restoration. Similarly, the Philistines are to be destroyed because of their perpetual enmity (25: 15). These four peoples, it will be noticed, Ammon, Moab, Edom and Philistia, are those in immediate contact with Israel, and their destruction or reduction to powerlessness is a necessary political step to Israel's undisturbed enjoyment of her own land.

From them we pass to Tyre, which receives much more attention, covering nearly three chapters, followed by a brief appendix on Sidon. The reason for this is, no doubt, that Tyre was very much on the front page of the news after the fall of Jerusalem when Nebu-

[1] Ammon seized Judean territory after 586.

chadrezzar went on to besiege it. Tyre also is accused of "Schadenfreude", malicious joy, at the downfall of Jerusalem, since caravan-tolls will no longer be paid to her. Therefore Yahweh has brought up Nebuchadrezzar to besiege Tyre in her island fortress, and to overthrow her mainland dependencies. Her downfall and political extinction are prophesied, though as a matter of history this prophecy was not fulfilled; after a siege of thirteen years, the result was inconclusive. The effect of the imagined overthrow on the surrounding peoples is described at length by the prophet (26: 15 ff.). In Chapter 27 there is a lament over Tyre in the regular metre of a dirge which is usually regarded as one of the finest of Ezekiel's poems. The allegory is that of a stately ship, overtaken by a storm and wrecked, and gives a vivid picture of ancient shipbuilding and equipment. The poem is interrupted by the prose passage of verses 12–25 describing the trade of Tyre; this should be omitted in reading the poem, since it is clearly, both in form and substance, an interpolation. The dirge ends with an included dirge, sung by the women of the onlookers:

> *Who has been ruined like Tyre*
> *in the heart of the sea?*
> *When your merchandise came from the seas*
> *you supplied many peoples;*
> *With the abundance of your wealth and your wares*
> *you enriched the kings of the earth.*
> *Now you are wrecked in the seas,*
> *in the depth of the waters;*
> *Your cargo and all your crew*
> *are sunk in the heart of you.*

> (vv. 32 ff.)

The following Chapter (28) contains two oracles against the King of Tyre, as the representative of the city (Ithobaal II). He is denounced for pride and arrogance,

nurtured by the great prosperity of Tyre. He has said
in effect:

> *I am a god,*
> *I sit in the seat of the gods*
> *In the heart of the seas.*

though he is but a man and no god, on whom destruction is coming. The same theme is continued in a second
oracle (11-19), which many readers find the most difficult in the book, because of its use of ancient mythology.
The myth runs parallel with that of Adam, in that it
describes one who dwells in Eden, the garden of God,
in glorious beauty and with all that heart could desire.
Then came the fall, brought about by the very prosperity and pride in it; this angelic being is expelled from
the garden by the very cherubim which were his guards.
So shall it be with the King of Tyre:

> *You were puffed up with pride through your beauty*
> *You ruined your wisdom by reason of your splendour.*

The obscurities and corruptions of the Massoretic text
have made the passage unnecessarily difficult, especially
its identification of the glorious being with his cherubic
guardians in verses 14 and 16:

> *Thou wast the anointed cherub that covereth*
> *and I set thee. . . .*

which gives no sense in its context. The Septuagint and
Syriac seem to have read simply (*eth* for *att*) "With the
cherub I set thee", which gives a good sense. (The
addition of "anointed" and "that covereth" may be due
to confusion with the cherubim of the ark and their
covering wings.) So, in verse 16:

> *I have destroyed thee: O covering cherub*

the Septuagint again helps us to the true sense, since it reads

The cherub led thee out.

These details illustrate the fate of the text of Ezekiel. The obscurities of subject-matter have invited further obscurities of text, so that the ordinary reader can often make nothing of the rendering in our Authorized or Revised Versions, just because they follow the Hebrew only.

After the brief oracle against Sidon (21–23), this group of prophecies is summed up by the remark (24) that Israel will no longer suffer from its neighbours, and that (25, 26) they will then have secure prosperity in their own land to which Yahweh will have restored them. The judgment on the nations has this ultimate purpose of restoration in view, besides the immediate one of retribution.

The remaining four chapters of foreign oracles are wholly devoted to Egypt. Apart from Babylon, she was the only great imperial power on Ezekiel's horizon, and Babylon is not denounced by him, because she is regarded as the avenging sword in the hand of Yahweh. The end of Egypt, like that of Israel's other neighbours, is destruction, or at least reduction to utter helplessness. The charge against her is:

Because you have been a staff of reed
To the house of Israel—
When they grasped you by the hand, you snapped,
And tore all their hand;
And when they leaned upon you, you broke,
And made all their loins quake.

(29: 6, 7.)

That charge is justified by history. Throughout the

struggle for world-power between the peoples of the Nile and of the Tigris-Euphrates river civilizations, Egypt was again and again the false or ineffective friend of Israel, inciting her to rebellion, as a pawn in the political game, against the Mesopotamian power. We have a curious example of "Real-Politik" in the realm of theology in the promise that the capture of Egypt by Nebuchadrezzar shall be his compensation for the ultimate failure to capture Tyre (29: 18, 19):

> As a return for the campaign which he directed against Tyre, I am giving him the land of Egypt, because they rendered a service to me.

We know that Nebuchadrezzar did set out to invade Egypt after raising the siege of Tyre, but there is no evidence of his permanent occupation of it, or of any such fate befalling Egypt as these prophecies foretell.

The first of the oracles aptly compares Pharaoh with a great crocodile taken and cast ashore to be the prey of beasts and birds. Another oracle (30: 20-26) describes the breaking of Pharaoh's arm, with triple repetition, suggesting that editors have gathered and put together three forms of the same prophecy. Yet another uses the allegory of a stately tree, with its root by many waters, which shall lie overthrown with broken branches, left to the birds and the beasts. These and other figures describe the desolation which shall befall the land when the sword of the King of Babylon (31: 11) shall descend upon it. In one place it is said that the desolation will endure for forty years, during which the Egyptians will be scattered amongst the nations, before they are brought back to humble political existence. This may be suggested by Israel's forty years in the desert.

The climax of this cycle of anti-Egyptian prophecies is found in the impressive picture of Sheol in Chapter 32. Here Egypt joins the great array of peoples and empires which have passed away, and is hailed by her predecessors, much as the unnamed tyrant of Isaiah 14 is scornfully welcomed to Sheol. Ezekiel catalogues the powers of the ancient world with which Israel has had to do—the Assyrians, whose empire had fallen last of them all, in 612, within the prophet's memory; Elam, and other powers. It is emphasized that Egypt the circumcized must lie with all these uncircumcized people, a characteristic Jewish touch. Sheol is not yet, of course, a place of penalty, but it marks the futile end of earthly ambition for empires as for individual men. As the old Song of Deborah ended, so might the prophet here have said:

> *Thus may all Thine enemies perish, Yahweh,*
> *But let Thy friends be like the rising of the sun in his might.*

Before we leave the subject of the judgment on the nations, which cleared the way for Israel's restoration as Ezekiel conceived it, we ought to notice the prophecy of the overthrow of Gog in Chapters 38 and 39, though this eschatological passage is now generally regarded as later than Ezekiel. Here we have passed quite beyond the contemporary politics of Ezekiel's day as closely interwoven with his oracles as are Guelph and Ghibelline politics with Dante's poem. Gog from the land of Magog, at the head of his northern hosts, cannot be identified with any historical figure, nor can his land be geographically located. He is a figure of mystery, incorporating the final outbreak of heathenism upon God's people. In him, all the old enmities come to a head, that they may be once and for all destroyed. So he marches against an Israel restored to its land, and dwelling in security; but he marches only to meet defeat by the supernatural forces which Yahweh hurls upon him. It will take seven months to bury the dead, and the wood of their weapons will provide firewood for seven years. The purpose of it all is that men may know Yahweh,

the God of Israel, and understand for ever that it was not
His weakness but His strong justice, which brought
Israel into exile for their iniquity:

> Thus will I manifest My glory among the nations; and all
> the nations shall see the judgments that I execute and the
> hand that I lay upon them.

3. *The Restoration of Israel*

Ezekiel, whilst in Palestine, had pictured a righteous
remnant, marked on their foreheads with the sign of a
cross (X). But the future of Israel, as Ezekiel later conceives it, lies wholly with the exiles, and not with the
survivors in Judaea, who seem to have set up a claim
that the future was with them; for he quotes them as
saying (33: 24):

> Abraham was but one man, yet he received possession of
> the land; now we, being many, the land will surely be
> given to us as a possession.

We know, indeed, from the biography of Jeremiah, that
the Babylonians set up a government under Gedaliah
(40: 5) with whom Jeremiah remained. But Gedaliah
was assassinated through a conspiracy headed by Ishmael
of Davidic stock (2 Kings 25: 25; Jer. 41: 1). His rising
was suppressed by other Jews under Johanan, but these
themselves migrated to Egypt, compelling Jeremiah to
accompany them. Jeremiah himself had set his hopes for
the future on the Babylonian exiles, not on the Judaean
survivors, after 597, and had called the former the good
figs and the latter the bad figs in his vision of the two
baskets (24: 1 ff.).

It is significant that the two prophets agree in this
verdict, and history largely confirmed them, since the
actual stimulus to rebuild the temple in 520 seems to
have come from Babylon, not from "the people of the

land". But Ezekiel extends his view from the exiles in Babylon to include those from the northern kingdom, "the lost tribes", beloved of British Israelites. His symbolic action of lying on his side had prescribed a limit to their exile, as well as to that of Judah (4: 4–6), and in the later symbolism of the two sticks (37: 15–28) joined together, he foresaw the reunion of the two kingdoms under a single ruler.

How these scattered exiles are to be gathered after the "forty years", the generation of exile, Ezekiel cannot tell us. In this he differs very markedly from Deutero-Isaiah, who, about the middle of the century, saw in the Persian Cyrus the anointed of Yahweh who would overthrow Babylon and enable the exiles to return. But circumstances were different then and it was possible to see the hand of God actually at work in current events. Ezekiel is thrown back on the miracle of divine intervention, aptly suggested in his vision of the valley of dry bones, and "supernaturalism", so characteristic of his theology, does not fail him. In Chapter 36: 8 he says of Israel that they shall shortly come back to their land. His last dated prophecy, that promising Egypt to Nebuchadrezzar, falls in April of 571, twenty years before Cyrus came to the front.

But Ezekiel atones for his ignorance as to the occasion of the restoration by giving us much more information concerning the restored State. He is expectant, as we have just seen, of a single State, under "my servant David" (34: 23; 37: 24, 25) who is to be prince for ever, an ideal ruler recalling the golden age of the first David. In this connection, we note that he is called "prince" (nasi), not king. Ezekiel, in fact, follows Hosea in denouncing the actual kings of Israel; they are called "Shepherds" in Chapter 34. They have sought their own ends, and the flock has accordingly suffered; the failure of the shepherds has led to the scattering of the sheep. In the latter part of the chapter (from 17) the difference of the good and bad sheep within the flock is developed. In Chapter 34 we have the picture of God as the good shepherd seeking out His scattered sheep (12 ff.).

The land itself is addressed in Chapter 36 under the phrase "mountains of Israel". The land has borne the reproach of the nations (36: 6) as being a devourer of men (13), a mother of famine, not of plenty (30). All that will be removed in the restored State:

> I will make the fruit of the trees and the produce of the fields abundant, so that ye may no longer bear among the nations the reproach of famine.
>
> (30).

This increase of fruitfulness is a constant feature of descriptions of the future, the heaven on earth which will be the fulfilment of the expected kingdom of God. For it is God's kingdom that is at last to be realized, and the prince, its visible head, is clearly only His deputy. The land itself is redivided amongst the twelve tribes (47: 13–48: 35), but the division, as we shall see, is wholly Utopian, and is such as a child might make with a ruler upon the map, without any regard to the natural divisions, the topography which makes actual history.

The central and primary interest of this restored State is the temple, and the detailed attention given to this in the closing chapters of the book raises points of importance and of permanent interest, and justifies us in regarding Ezekiel as the most sacramentally minded of the prophets. The temple is, in fact, the final end of Israel's existence, the final proof of its election (37: 26–8):

> I will set My sanctuary in the midst of them forever, and My dwelling-place shall be with them; and I will be their God and they shall be My people. And when My sanctuary is set in the midst of them forever, the nations shall know that I Yahweh am setting Israel apart for Myself.

The last nine chapters of the Book of Ezekiel are in the form of a vision, dated 573, which describes the future temple, its ministry and maintenance and some features of its worship. Considerable parts of it read more like the Book of Leviticus than a prophet's vision, and the disproportionate character of some of the detail has convinced many modern students of the book that large additions have been made to whatever Ezekiel originally wrote. But points of literary criticism, as well as those of merely antiquarian interest, such as the rules for sacerdotal hairdressing (44: 20), do not here concern us. It should be noted, however, that some of these points are important for the history of the development of Israel's religion. Thus we notice that the priesthood is confined to Zadokites only, that is, to the priests who functioned in the temple in the pre-exilic period; the priests of the pre-Deuteronomic local sanctuaries are degraded to non-priestly Levites (43: 19). An interesting passage describes the general function of the priest as Ezekiel conceived it (44: 3 f.):

> They shall teach My people the difference between the sacred and the secular, and show them how to distinguish between the unclean and the clean. In a case at court they shall act as judges, and shall decide the case according to My laws, and they shall observe My rules and regulations at all my festivals, and shall maintain the sacredness of My sabbaths.

The ancient function of the priest, to give "revelation" by the sacred lot, the original "Torah", is still apparent, though, as the keeper of tradition and precedent, the priest has now become a regular legal authority (alongside of the lay jurisdiction of the "elders"). The priest is obviously much more than a sacrificer, though by Ezekiel's time he has naturally become the specialist in sacrifice.

The secular power of the prince is minimized; in fact, he seems to have little more to do than to oversee the provision for the sacrifices, as a sort of ecclesiastical commissioner (45: 7 ff., 17 ff.). Beside the two main types of pre-exilic sacrifice, the peace-offering and the burnt-offering, there now appear the sin-offering and the guilt-offering (44: 29; 40: 39, 42), so prominent in the post-exilic religion. In regard to the festivals, we have noticed the priestly duty to enforce sabbath observance, another difference from pre-exilic conceptions of it. The festival days are divided between the first and the seventh month, i.e. they come half-yearly (45: 20 ff.). The spring festival is that of Passover-Mazzoth, the autumn festival that of Tabernacles; Ezekiel makes no mention of Pentecost. Nor does he make mention of the observance which was to hold so great a place in later Judaism, the Day of Atonement on the tenth of the seventh month; his nearest approach to it is two annual observances for expiation on the first day of the first and seventh months (45: 18 ff.).

The dominating principle of all that is said is tersely expressed in Chapter 42: 20. It is to separate the sacred from the secular. Definite objection is taken to the old order of the Solomonic temple, in which the temple was virtually a royal chapel (43: 7 ff.):

> The house of Israel shall no longer defile My holy name, neither they nor their kings by their idolatry and by the dead bodies of their kings, by placing their threshold against My threshold, and their doorpost against My doorpost, with only a wall between Me and them.

So we find there is to be new planning of the temple and of Jerusalem to avoid this juxtaposition. The temple in the centre is insulated by the priests around it, and the Levites to the north of them, whilst the changed site of the city is now to the south of the priests. Northwards in parallel strips extend Judah, Reuben, Ephraim, Manasseh, Naphtali, Asher, and Dan; southwards of the city, Benjamin, Simeon, Issachar, Zebulun, Gad. The order is significant, the "concubine" tribes being the more remote, but the whole scheme is Utopian, even though so much realism of detail is now mingled with it.

This mingling of the ideal and the real is seen also in the one passage of this section of the book which attracts the general reader, viz. the account of the life-bringing stream which flows from the temple eastward to enter the Dead Sea and give it life. Yet the marshes and swamps are still to remain salt—in order to provide the supply of salt for the temple sacrifices (47: 11)!

The reason for all these changes is obvious. It is to make the new temple and the changed land a fitting environment for Him whose glorious presence the prophet sees returning to His home, even as he had seen that same glory leaving it, in the old idolatrous days (43: 1-4; cf. 11: 22-5). Henceforth, the name of the city will be—and this is the closing word of the book—"Yahweh is there". That is the characteristic sacramentalism of Ezekiel, which stands as the fitting accompaniment of his supernaturalism. The holy God will find a worthy mediation of His glory and His presence through holy worship.

As we review our study of the Book of Ezekiel, we may be more conscious of its shortcomings and limitations than of its achievements We miss the glowing evangelism of Deutero-Isaiah; the sense of a message of grace to all peoples which is to be mediated through Israel as the Servant of Yahweh. We can hardly help feeling that Ezekiel's God is too much concerned with His own honour and too little with the good of man. We cannot feel that the wholesale destruction of Israel's enemies, even to vindicate the good name of

God, is worthy of Him. A more difficult and more glorious task belongs to Him in the conversion of enemies into friends, and to this Ezekiel makes no contribution. Yet we must not lose sight of the prophet's faith that could see a new temple rising from the ruins of the old, nor of his recognition that the regenerating spirit of God alone could create a new and true Israel. Israel had a mission to the world for it was to be the means by which Yahweh would be known to all men. If we judge Ezekiel, as we ought, by his place in history, and not by standards of higher revelation, we can see how necessary was his particular form of faith for an Israel not yet ready to inherit the higher hopes of Deutero-Isaiah. That is the reason why he has been called the father of Judaism, with its virtues and its vices; that is why he has exerted so much influence on the subsequent generations of Israel. Idealism is the salt of religion, but there must be something to salt and it was this that Ezekiel's realism so strikingly recognized and worked out.